HOTDOGS FOR HYENAS

A Soul Forged in Rhodesia

Pamela Courtney

HOME HOUSE PRESS
An Imprint of United Writers Press
CHARLESTON, S.C.

Hotdogs for Hyenas
by Pamela Courtney

All rights reserved. No part of this book may be used in any form or reproduced by any means without written permission from the publisher with the exception of brief passages quoted in reviews, critical articles, or essays.

Copyright © 2021 by Pamela Courtney

ISBN: 978-1-952248-82-5

Published by

HOME
HOUSE
PRESS

AN IMPRINT OF UNITED WRITERS PRESS

109 Broad Street
Charleston, S.C. 29401

Printed in the U.S.A.

Dedicated to
Graham David "Bob" and Denise Gawler
and
Jimius Ndlovu

CONTENTS

SPECIAL THANKS VII
FOREWORD IX
GLOSSARY XI
TIMELINE OF RHODESIA XIII

INTRODUCTION 1

PART 1
1. HOT DOGS FOR HYENAS 11
2. CHANGE FOREVER 29

PART 2
3. THE BIG MOVE 43
4. MISSION SITE NUMBER 1 67
5. LOSING MISSION NUMBER 1 69
6. MISSION SITE NUMBER 2 79
7. LOSING MISSION NUMBER 2 95
8. MISSION SITE NUMBER 3 101
9. LOSING MISSION NUMBER 3 119

PART 3
10. MY FAVORITE SNAKE STORIES 129
11. HUNTING 141
12. EDUCATION 155
13. LESSONS IN RESILIENCE 165
14. THE POWER OF NGANGA 177
15. TERRORISM CROSSES ALL BOUNDARIES 185

PART 4
16. REENTRY INTO AMERICA 189
17. ATTACK ON MY MOTHER 203
18. GOING BACK HOME TO VISIT 213
19. FINAL THOUGHTS 223

EPILOGUE 233

ACKNOWLEDGMENTS 237
   BOB AND DENISE GAWLER 237
   JIMILIS NDLOVU 241

BIBLIOGRAPHY 245
ABOUT THE AUTHOR 247

SPECIAL THANKS TO:

Licia, Gavin and Joni for your expertise, input and sympatico of this project. Tom and Vally for opening the doors for crucial edits and publishing. Alan, for your continual support. The breakfast club members, Sam, Glen, Bill, Jerry, Tommy, Warren, James, Matt, Jennifer and Grant. The finest group to interact with every morning. To the staff employee who handed me a pink sticky note that said, "iPam" commenting, "You support everyone here, we want to know you. Please write your book." I still have the sticky note.

The entire Reynolds family, who have been so inclusive on every level. Steve who read, reread, counseled, and pushed me through the most difficult times of writing. When I felt I was moving through a minefield of memories unsure I wanted to expose, you gave me the why and shared tears when I read the last word. My well-grounded children, Thomas and Summer, daughter-in-law Bethany, tender grandchildren, Grayson, and Charlotte. You gave me the most coveted role in life, momma and ouma. And to my parents, who loved me fiercely and instilled the key word in my life: resilience!

FOREWORD

I met Pam in Washington, D.C. in 1984 and, through her introductions, subsequently worked at the South African Embassy in Washington, D.C. I set up the Media Monitoring and Analysis Center in the Department of Press and Information, remaining in that role through the F.W. de Klerk / Nelson Mandela presidential transition. That position morphed into my being the Protocol Officer for the U.S.A-South Africa Binational Commission.

If life is a safari and the journey is the reward, Pamela Courtney certainly fits the mold. Rhodesians were an adaptive breed, as are all Zimbabweans today. Africa, in general, delivers a rugged reality and its own romantic charm. To live in Africa, one certainly feels the adventure of life come alive in his soul. Pam's memoirs of living in Rhodesia—now Zimbabwe—take you there. Her tales span half a century, from the 1960s through the bush war in Rhodesia to 9/11.

Pamela takes you on the personal safari of one who has experienced being born or raised in Africa and experienced the additional adventure of living outside the continent. Those of us like her will read this book with nostalgia for both the simplicity and the rugged endurance of the journey. There is an inspiring bond between those who have bridged life from the African bush to the American highway—or any other Western civilization.

From being thrown off a horse when a leopard jumps in front of her and negotiating the tightwire between the power of witchdoctors and the missionary work of a church to returning to the United States to attend university and adjusting to unexpected culture shock—this book has it all. At the close of the final chapter, you will most certainly feel Pam's experience of living in full exploration, inwardly seeking

HOTDOGS for HYENAS

awareness, finding answers, reflecting…and finally inspiring others to go on soul adventures of their own.

So, put your feet up and enjoy a good read.

Gavin McLeman
Fellow Rhodesian and
Zimbabwe-American

GLOSSARY

Baba – Father
Bietjie – Little Beast
Biltong – Bulls tongue – dried meat
Boeremeisie – Farm girl
Boetie – Brother
Braai (Braaivleis) – Cookout
Bundu – Bush
Chisikana – Girl
Chiremba – Doctor
Dine River (pronounced Dee-nee) – River close to the mission
Doro – Beer
Guti – Light misty rain
Knobkerrie – long handled club with rounded head
Kopje – (pronounced Cop-pee) – Rock outcropping
Kraal – Enclosure
Lekker – (Baie lekker) - Delicious, very delicious, but can be used to describe anything great
Lorry – Truck
Lowveld – Area in the southern region of Rhodesia/Zimbabwe
Maize – Mealies (a white field corn)
Meisie – Girl
Mooshie – Absolutely great
Monga – Millet type seed
Mopani – Hardwood tree plentiful throughout the bush
Muti – Medicine
Ndaba – Discussion
Nganga – Healer (used to describe a witchdoctor)
Nuanetsi (now Mwenzi) – River close to the mission. Also name of the police station.
Rutanga – Railroad Siding 50 miles from mission
Sadza – Staple diet made from the maize/mealies
Umfundisi – Teacher
Veldschoens (vellies) – Suede lace-up shoes
Voetsak – Get away

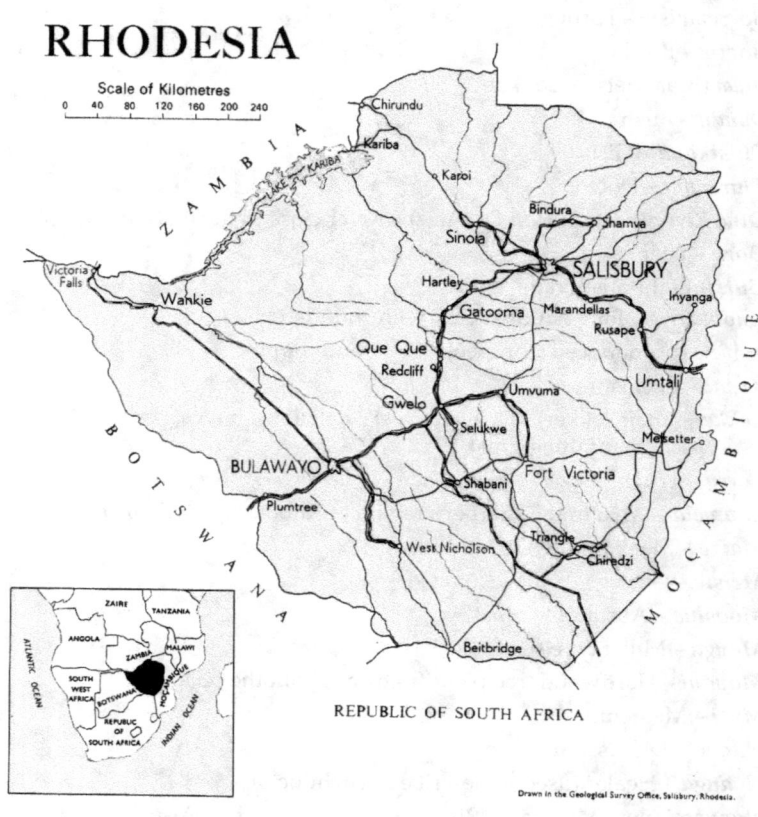

TIMELINE OF RHODESIA

2 million years ago: Homo erectus, a bipedal hominoid, originates in Africa.

200,000 BCE: Neanderthals emigrate from southern Africa.

50,000 BCE: Homo sapiens (Adam and Eve) originates in southern Africa.

20,000 – 10,600 BCE: Ice Age, Africa is lush, tropical.

12,800 BCE: First of series of catastrophic events in northern America impacts climate (massive solar ejection, meteor, comet, or asteroid) and causes melting of glaciers, global cooling and resumption of the Ice Age.

10,600 BCE: The last large impact ends the Ice Age; ocean levels rise 140 meters (420 feet)

10,000 BCE: In Great Zimbabwe, stone circle construction begins. Adams Calendar created, signaling advanced astronomical knowledge.

700 CE: Arabians and Persians trade ivory, rhino horn, gold, shells, and slaves.

1000: Shona people begin their rule and occupy a city they call Zimbabwe (Great Stone House).

1400s: The Karanga branch of the Shona establishes the Mwanamutapa Empire.

1500s: The Rowzi branch rebels and forms Changamire Empire; Christianity is introduced by Portuguese explorers.

1531: The first written record of the Great Zimbabwe ruins is created by Vincente Pegado.

1830s: The Nguni people from the south defeat the empire.

1855: November 17: Dr. David Livingston, missionary and explorer, becomes the first European to see Victoria Falls.

1873: May 1: Dr. David Livingston dies in modern-day Zambia of malaria and internal bleeding.

1888: Lobengula, king of the Matebele, signs an agreement that grants mineral rights to the Cecil John Rhodes / British South African Company.

1890: The Pioneer Column arrives, settling the town of Salisbury (Harare).

1893: The British South African Company occupies the region and calls the territory Rhodesia.

1893, July: Matebele War—Lobengula's warriors raid British settlers near Fort Victoria (Masvingo); Great Britain responds with force until Rhodesia is under British control.

1897: Great Britain recognizes Southern and Northern Rhodesia as separate territories.

1902: March 26: Cecil John Rhodes dies and is buried at Matopos in Rhodesia.

1923: Southern Rhodesia becomes a self-governing British colony.

1953: Great Britain sets up the Federation of Rhodesia and Nyasaland, which includes the territories of Southern and Northern Rhodesia.

HOTDOGS for HYENAS

1963/1964: The Federation of Rhodesia and Nyasaland is dissolved; Northern Rhodesia becomes Zambia, Nyasaland becomes Malawi, and Southern Rhodesia becomes Rhodesia (now Zimbabwe).

1965, November 11: Rhodesian Prime Minister Ian Smith declares Rhodesia independent; Great Britain declares independence illegal, banning trade with Rhodesia; the Rhodesian Bush War begins.

1966: The United Nations imposes sanctions on Rhodesia.

1969: A new constitution is introduced to prevent black Africans from gaining control of the government.

1970, March 2: Rhodesia declares itself a republic.

1977: Prime Minister Smith begins to make plans to establish a new government with a majority of black leaders.

1979: April: Abel T. Muzorewa becomes the first black prime minister.

1979, May 31: Zimbabwe proclaims independence.

1979, June 1: The nation of Zimbabwe, formerly Rhodesia, is formed.

1980, April 18: Great Britain recognizes the country's independence; Rhodesia's name is officially changed to Zimbabwe.

1980-1987: Robert Mugabe serves as Prime Minister of Zimbabwe:

1983-1987: Robert Mugabe's Gukurahundi (torture and mass murder of Ndebele people

1987-2017: Robert Mugabe serves as President of Zimbabwe

2017, November 19: Coup d'etat. Dictator Robert Mugabe is ousted from power after 37 years in power.

The Call of Africa

C. Emily Dibb

When you have acquired a taste for the dust,
and the scent of our first rain,
You're hooked for life on Africa,
and you'll not be right again.

Until you can watch the setting moon
and hear the jackals bark,
And know they are around you
waiting in the dark.

When you long to see the elephants
or hear the coucal's song,
When the moonrise sets your blood on fire,
then you've been away too long.

It is time to cut the traces loose,
and let your heart go free,
Beyond that far horizon
where your spirit yearns to be.

Africa is waiting – come!
Since you have touched the open sky
And learned to love the rustling grass
and the wild fish eagle's cry.

You'll always hear the hunger for the bush;
for the lion's rasping roar,
To camp at last beneath the stars
and to be at peace once more.

Pamela Courtney's father in front of their first home in the bush. Board across the front was to keep snakes out. They cooked over the open fire and the "dining room" bench can be seen next to hut wall. Water was trucked in from 140 miles away.

INTRODUCTION

For years I intended to share the stories of being raised in the primitive African bush (in Rhodesia, now Zimbabwe) by missionary parents in the mid-twentieth century. The indelible imprint was begging to find a vehicle for exposure. Only those who lived it can understand the impact of living with a family unit so passionately inspired. The dangers were real.

But when I would clear my desk to begin writing, the project seemed too enormous and emotional. The pain was too fresh. I always put it off until "next year." Even though I worked for the embassy of South Africa and was on several speakers' bureaus, outside of my vocational commitments, my priorities were being with my family, raising children, and staying active in the horse industry. I spent time on the fast track as a magazine editor and a general manager and then went into the magazine publishing arena. I wrote feature stories and had a monthly column, but Africa was a topic I never found the opportunity to unleash.

In 2000, my expertise in cross-cultural concepts was recognized, and I was hired by Lenoir-Rhyne University as director of the Building Community from Diversity program, with the added responsibility of being the executive director of the Multicultural Center of Western North Carolina. Whether speaking or teaching, I generally slipped a few anecdotal African stories in with my lectures but still never wrote *the book*. In 2001, I returned to South Africa for the first time in a decade (since the black majority emancipation) to attend the UN Conference on Racism as an NGO representative. I was inspired to write about the experience but again never summoned the resolve.

A few years later, I returned to graduate school and, during my studies, presented a paper: "The Struggle for Gender Equality in Zimbabwe." While writing the paper, I spent several days at the Library of Congress in Washington, D.C., researching what had been published on the topic.

That's when the concept crystallized. It was apparent that I was far better versed on the disparities suffered by African women in Zimbabwe than the "expert" authors. I had firsthand experience in addition to personal stories to substantiate my opinions. During the presentation of my paper, I shared the drama of beatings women received from their families if they were stricken with the AIDS virus (usually acquired from their unfaithful husbands). I fast-forwarded to the active and dangerous roles Zimbabwean women played in the struggle for independence only to find themselves marginalized as inconsequential participants.

After I presented my paper, I opened the discussion to questions from the audience. I was woefully disappointed. The first question came from the chair of the department, who was evidently hungry to learn about the horrors of female circumcision. At the time, that topic was the only "newsworthy" subject being raised by the media about women in Africa. I hadn't even mentioned female circumcision.

To my audience, Zimbabwe was an abstract topic. African countries were lumped together, all having seemingly identical cultures. What a narrow-minded oversimplification. But no one shared or understood my passion about the calamity of a once-great nation, the breadbasket of Africa, now reduced to third-world status.

Fast-forward to 2015. I had begun co-authoring a book with one of my fellow missionary kids (Alan Smith, M.D.) about some of our hilarious exploits growing up in the African bush. While some of the recollections were of life-threatening occurrences, we intentionally

INTRODUCTION

wanted to keep our tales on the light side. I had buried my family's story deep in the recesses of my mind and had suppressed memories of a journey that could have destroyed my entire family. We let life and work sublimate our enthusiasm for writing.

Thanksgiving 2019 was set to be as comfortable as the woolen sweaters Mum used to knit in the bush. Tightly woven, cozy and nearly indestructible. I told my parents not to worry about the food, that I'd bring everything. My parents, in their mid-90s needed a little spoiling.

Descended from the community of Courtenay, France with later generations making their way to England in 1066, then to Virginia in the early 1600s, part of Dad's family experienced the great migration of the late 1700s. The family settled in the mountains of East Tennessee for the next 100 years before trekking west.

Dad was born in Colorado. His mother was a second-grade schoolteacher. His father, a landowner and farmer, had his own academic career stunted when he walked a cow up the stairs of the belfry tower of his school.

While still in grade school, Dad became fascinated with flying. He was known to be a bit of a daydreamer. No one was surprised when the school bus ran over his foot because his attention was on a biplane making passes over a cornfield. His love for horses also developed at this time. He spent hours in the saddle, rounding up horses on the family's Colorado ranches. By the time Dad reached high school he was tall, lanky, played basketball, but his health was always an issue. Re-occurrences of pneumonia had already had a lasting effect on his lungs. The family was advised he needed to be moved to a more accommodating climate.

They moved to the breadbasket of Oregon, the Willamette Valley during his high school years. His sights were set on pre-med. Although raised in a devotedly Baptist home, attending church regularly, he had no notion of the mission field.

Mum, on the other hand, the second youngest of six children, descended on her dad's side from one of the first wagonmasters to lead families through treacherous conditions to the Oregon territory. Her mother, grandparents, and great-grandparents immigrated from Norka, Russia.

Raised in an agnostic home, Mum began attending church during her last year of high school. It was then she dreamed of becoming a missionary and helping others. She enrolled in college with her sights set on a 5-year Bachelor of Theology degree.

She did not go to college to find a husband, but she got both the theology degree and her mate for life. Dad turned around in class and laid eyes on this tiny black-haired cheerleader who had a skirt over her knees. They were married shortly after, but continued their studies at University of Oregon, Northwest Christian University, and Willamette University. They sold their car, bought a Harley and spent their off-time exploring America, Canada, and Mexico. With a pup tent and a one-burner stove they learned to rely on one another from the beginning. When going to work at the hospital, Mum would ride side saddle on the bike in order not to wrinkle her starched white uniform. On one of the jaunts down Mt. Hood, Oregon, Dad kept dropping the bike due to icy road conditions. Mum threatened to walk all the way down without him. She was his anchor.

Now, with nearly 76 years of marriage under their belts, I was joining them for Thanksgiving. I called ahead to Cracker Barrel in northern Florida for our feast and started the drive from South Carolina. I arrived right on time at my parents' small, immaculately-groomed farm and unloaded the turkey, dressing, green beans, and sweet potatoes. My mother had already set the table and insisted on making the gravy. Dad was already at his chair. As I walked in, he turned his head up and gave me a big kiss and hug. This was the first time we'd celebrated this holiday together in years.

Growing up in Africa, Thanksgiving wasn't celebrated, and I'd never really become accustomed to it. I'd purchased a tablecloth and wanted to begin a new tradition to hand down to my daughter. After dinner, Dad, Mum and I signed the tablecloth as a remembrance of this special time. My intent was to embroider the signatures.

INTRODUCTION

After we cleared the table and were enjoying our pie and coffee, I looked on the wall at the enormous spoon collection that my mother had accrued. Each spoon represented a country we had visited. So many memories and stories, yet neither one of my parents had written about them. Dad had kept a small diary for a short period, but that was it. My mother was too busy with life to take the time to indulge in the luxury of writing a book. I'd wished they had because I was so young when arriving in Africa, I surely missed so much.

We continued to stay gathered around the table, Dad asking Mum to retrieve photos of Africa. She had several wrapped and clipped together. Many had her neat and precise handwriting separating the photos into categories. With each photo my parents shared a story. We talked for nearly eight hours. I asked for a couple of photos to keep. I finally excused myself to go to bed.

Around 3 a.m. I heard pounding on the front door. It wouldn't stop. I got up and could see there was no outside light on. An uncontrollable shiver engulfed my body. I was thrown into Africa mode. My fear factor kicked in. My parents had a front gate that was always closed, and they controlled the remote that provided access to the house. I knew if I opened the door, someone would rush in, robbing us or even worse. They probably knew an elderly couple lived here and it was the holidays.

I finally said, "Who's there?"

They responded, "The police. We received a 911 call from inside the house."

I highly doubted it, figuring this was a ploy for me to open the door. I asked, "How did you get over the gate?" The officers responded that they had jumped the gate. I stepped into Dad's office to look out the window. At that moment, I saw the blue lights just on the outside of the gate. I opened the front door.

About that time, my mother came around the corner to the front hall where I was standing. At 96, the ravages of osteoporosis had reduced her to 4'9"; her eyes were wide with terror.

"What has Tom done now?" she asked.

The officers again stated they had received a call from inside the house. I told them to step inside. They said a Dr. Courtney called saying a woman claiming to be his daughter was in the house and sleeping in the guest room. He didn't know if this was his true daughter and asked them to come immediately.

I was numb. What was going on? They informed me they had run the tags on the vehicle I was driving and next asked to see my license. I led one officer into the guest bedroom and after digging through my purse handed him my license, assuring him I was their daughter. I then stepped into the living room and could see Dad, shirtless, sitting at the kitchen table talking with the other officer. I walked to the table and the two officers said, "We can assure you that Miss Pamela is your daughter."

"Well, you can never be too sure," said Dad.

I walked the officers to the door. They asked me if there were guns in the house. I looked at them and said, "My family is from Africa—this place is like an arsenal. I can assure you that the closet directly behind me has several weapons."

One of the officers looked at me, his expression solemn. "It's probably time for you to remove these weapons. Your dad may not recognize you at some point—or even your mother."

I was stunned. My dad, brilliant, read Greek every day, the hunter, the provider, the intellect, the pioneer, the fearless adventurer, the man who could do anything. He built a mission including a clinic with his bare hands!

I was slowly grasping what was happening. I was being asked to take guns out of the house because he might harm us. I went back to bed, but before I did, I locked the door to my room—not because of terrorists but because, for the first time in my life, I was afraid of sleeping in my parents' home. I lay down and thought of the character traits my parents had instilled in me, traits I would carry with me regardless of where I lived: (1) not acting like a spoiled American (the ugly American), (2) not talking down to people, regardless of their culture, (3) not building relationships based on money, and

INTRODUCTION

(4) always being kind—all qualities that speak volumes concerning personal character. What a fortunate daughter I was to be in my 60s and still have both my parents.

The next day, Mother and I drove into town. She apologized for what had happened.

"How long has this been going on?" I asked.

"About a year," she said.

I went through the normal questions of whether their doctor knew and if Dad was on Alzheimer's medication. All elicited a negative response. I asked for the name of their family doctor, but she wouldn't tell me. She would stand by her man "till death do us part." She harbored intense fear that Dad might be taken out of the home. She didn't know what to do.

I told her about the officer's advisement about the guns. She remained quiet all the way home. The next night I reached in the closet to begin removing the weapons. They were gone! I knew right there and then that they had probably been moved to the master bedroom. I knew, because of Dad's tremors, that his handling a rifle was probably unthinkable, but there were at least four handguns in the house.

My father—the one who had taught me gun safety—was close to having his weapons taken away *by his own daughter*. I returned to bed that night, once again locking my bedroom door. I just couldn't ask my mother to hand over the guns. She was still very much in control and protective of the man to whom she had been married for nearly eight decades.

The next day we chatted over coffee, never mentioning the incident of Dad's not remembering who I was. In early stages of dementia, perhaps he could not merge the adult woman sitting in his house with the one in the photographs spread across the table. I asked questions about our lives in the bush, making sure what I remembered was correct.

"Pam," said Dad, "we protected you so much, you probably only know half of what went on over there."

I began writing with the resolve not to quit. I would write only a few paragraphs at a time, not wanting to cross some difficult thresholds and stir up intensely painful recollections.

Churches in America have sent missionaries to all corners of the world and, in most circumstances, politics in the "mission field" do not cross their minds. Nor do jealousy, infidelity, narcissism, and the destruction of families for personal gain.

In the beginning of writing this book, I felt I was being pushed through a minefield, but it soon became apparent that I was, instead, being led down an important spiritual trail. For this reason, my story and my family's journey needs to be chronicled.

I am truly a "Third Culture Kid" — American by birth, but African by soul.

PART 1

1
HOT DOGS FOR HYENAS

In 1972, the war in Rhodesia was squarely in its eighth year (1964-1979), although there had been terrorist activities in some areas much longer. The ten-year civil war going on next door in Mozambique between Frelimo and Portugal was ending. Guerillas or terrorists being trained in Mozambique would flood over the border into Rhodesia for nightly raids, increasing the pucker factor — particularly for those of us living in rural areas.

But then, again, let's face it, most of Rhodesia was rural. And when I say rural, I don't mean the western concept of uniquely designed mailboxes hugging the road in front of three board fences with lazy overfed cows chewing their cud on sparkling green verdant pastures.

Rural meant bush veld. Rural meant 50 miles to the butcher shop. Rural meant 40 miles to the post office. Rural meant 18 miles to the nearest phone (and that was a crank phone tied into the police station 40 miles away). Rural meant 25 miles to the nearest neighbor. Rural meant you only went to town, Bulawayo (250 miles, 7 hours by truck), once a month for supplies. Rural meant you'd better plan ahead.

During the nightly raids, the terrorists oozing out of Mozambique would plant land mines inside Rhodesia. For so long we referred to terrorists as "terrors or tourists" because, we were convinced, they were traveling through and their nonsense would be over soon. Their public relations by bush telegraph (a term used to describe how messages are transmitted rapidly from person to person), stating that they were looking for small European children to cut into pieces and make an example of, worked well.

Robert Gabriel Mugabe (a Shona)—a shadowy figure we barely acknowledged—was a major leader behind this. We assumed this since the most notorious guerilla leader, Joshua Nkomo (from the Ndebele tribe), was under lock and key not far from our home. We would occasionally see photos of Nkomo at *Gonakudzingwa* strolling around the government internment compound. The photographer's lens seemed to always capture him wearing a light-colored blue shirt with his ample gut poking out between the buttons. Outsiders referred to his living conditions as a concentration camp.

"Not hardly," I thought. Nkomo was obese—a condition unheard of, considering the minimal diet of sadza (white mealie meal ground up and boiled) the rest of black Africans lived on. Nkomo strutted and preened his fat ass in front of cameras every chance he was given. We were on guard with him. He was the self-proclaimed leader of "majority rule."

But Mugabe? Hardly a household name—at least not in our household. Little did we imagine that, as events would unfold, Mugabe would push Nkomo to the side, crushing his influence, and ultimately decimate the region. Rhodesia, once a fertile food exporter throughout Africa, would be turned into the begging bowl of the world. That is the country I, the daughter of American missionaries, had grown up in.

But now it was 1972 and I was home from university. The day of final exams my sophomore year, I was already boarding a flight to London, with a connecting flight to Salisbury (now Harare). I'd suffered terrible bouts of homesickness while in the U.S. Towards the end of my sophomore year, I was walking down the hall of the dorm to my room when I overheard one of the cheerleaders whining on the pay phone. "I haven't been home for two months," she cried.

I raised my eyebrows unsympathetically. "I haven't been home in two years."

HOTDOGS FOR HYENAS

I would have sold my soul for the scent of the bush—the co-mingling of dust and dung.

Of course, too, there was the Vietnam War. Everyone on campus was focused on the war in southeast Asia. I occasionally would view the nightly news that showed rice paddies and helicopters, but I never really connected the dots. It all looked like the same footage to me—soldiers running through lots of dense green jungle towards awaiting helicopters.

The terrain looked nothing like the bush of Rhodesia. I rejoiced with my brother when he received a high lottery number, but that's about the limit of my engagement in trying to understand the U.S. fighting Mao on foreign soil. The "freedom fighter" bodies we would come across in the bush were also Chinese-trained. Somewhere on their bodies we would find medals with Mao's image on them.

Now *that* was real. That was in our back yards or in the maize fields we'd cut across on our way home.

The disconnect with me was stark. Students in America were concerned about a war on the opposite side of the planet from where they were living. Their day-to-day living conditions weren't exactly being threatened—they weren't under fire, they didn't have to carry a weapon when they went to get the mail as we did in the bush.

I'd come to university in 1970, knowing how to lock down a house, fire an FN (Fabrique Nationale) Belgian assault weapon used by European nations, keep an eye on potential harmful events to our household, and still put on a splendid tea, cocktail or dinner party as if nothing was rocking the stability of our tiny country.

I landed in Salisbury. It was June—winter in the southern hemisphere, 1,300 miles below the equator. As soon as the air hostess opened the hatch, the cool, fresh southern African air flooded the aircraft. I picked up my guitar and, when I stepped onto the rolling staircase, I looked straight out at the observation balcony.

I scanned for Mum and Dad and waved when I found them in the crowd. I was dressed fashionably in an off-white tunic and wool herringbone slacks. But my jacket screamed college student with the brown suede fringe dangling from the sleeves, back and bottom. The couple at whom I was waving intently looked straight through and beyond me, their eyes continuing to sweep to see who would emerge next from the plane. I walked across the tarmac.

"Mum! Dad!" I shouted. My parental unit turned their gaze towards me and, with little enthusiasm, waved at me, and continued looking behind me. I walked inside the terminal to clear customs, feeling uncertain that my parents knew me. Two years was an eternity and I missed them terribly.

The doors to the main terminal opened and it was a madhouse — wall to wall people. I could see Dad in a tweedy winter coat, one I recognized from when I was a little girl. I loved that coat because it had leather buttons — I'd chewed on them when I was a toddler — and because when I got close to the coat, it carried his scent, Old Spice.

As I approached my parents, I extended both my arms out, wrapping one arm around my mother, the other around my father. My parents still acted as if they were seeing me for the first time. I stood on my toes and kissed my dad, then my mother. She looked straight into my eyes. "Pamela, what have you done to your hair?" she said.

I could tell by the way the two of them were looking at me they were praying I'd say I was wearing a wig. "Uh, I dyed my hair."

That was an understatement. I'd gone to the hair salon and it had taken three dye jobs to transform my reddish-blonde hair to an understated shade of brown. My blonde eyebrows were a dead giveaway that I wasn't a brunette.

"It looks terrible," said Dad.

"What happened to my blonde daughter?" Mum said. "We'll have to fix that right away. We didn't even recognize you. We thought you were someone else's daughter."

We walked back outside to the tarmac. I shielded my eyes from the glare with an outstretched hand. Our turbo-charged Cessna 206, with its white and bronze paint, caught the rays of the sun. She was as beautiful as ever.

HOTDOGS FOR HYENAS

The Cessna had been a float plane. Dad had added an extra $6,000 in protective interior covering. Not necessary for a bush aircraft, but it was what Dad wanted. The plane had cost an astronomical amount of money. Back in the '60s, the purchase price had been nearly $50,000. A brand-new Chevy Impala cost only $2,500. But this six-seater was essential to survival in Africa, similar to those planes Alaskan bush pilots use today. Without roads and infrastructure, the only realistic form of travel was by air.

Mum opened the cargo doors and hopped in. Dad and I did a walk around and removed the chocks, and I opened the pilot/copilot door. There's a special smell that comes from a cockpit. Maybe it's a combination of vinyl seats and heat. Almost a toasty-smoky smell. If you've been in a light aircraft, you know what I'm talking about.

Pamela Courtney, age 17, with Cessna

HOTDOGS FOR HYENAS

Dad had already filed the flight plan and fueled the 85-gallon tanks. He looked at me. "It's all yours. Take us home."

I grabbed a booster pillow to prop under my butt, scanned the outside and yelled the pre-ignition pilot's standard warning, "Clear." I turned the key and the prop slowly turned over and effortlessly fired into life. I was in heaven.

I scanned the radio channel and frequency 078x and 113.1. I smiled as I keyed the mic. "Salisbury Control, this is Victor Papa Yankee Yankee Oscar."

A warm Rhodesia-accented voice responded, "Yankee Yankee Oscar, you are cleared to taxi to runway 05/23." After a few more directions from the tower, I advanced the throttle.

Would I overcompensate with the rudders? Would I remember what to do? At the threshold of the runway, I did a final pre-flight run-up to ensure all systems were ready for take-off. The tower cleared me for departure. I looked in the back. Mum was strapped in, already starting on some needlework project. Dad gave me a thumbs up. I completed the final checklist.

The runway at Salisbury was expansive, a full two miles long (and even now still one of the longest in southern Africa). Dad said, "You have lots of runway, but let's not use it all."

After takeoff, I climbed to 500 feet and banked to the left. The tower affectionately crackled. "Victor Papa Yankee Yankee Oscar, jolly good show. Welcome home." The mood was so cordial. We were valued. The controllers were an integral component of the infrastructure. With such limited roads, air traffic was essential to the economy, and we were frequent fliers.

We reached our cruising altitude of 11,000 feet. Dad confided into my intercom headphones, "You know you can request to fly higher if you want."

I laughed. "I don't feel like an ear-popping perilous descent today."

I had such an unnerving incident during high school flying from Johannesburg, South Africa to Rhodesia. We had climbed to 14,000 feet. Seated in the co-pilot's seat, with oxygen mask snuggly attached, I elected to take a little nap. After a while, Dad looked over from the pilot's seat and recognized I was in obvious distress — pale, limp and gasping for breath. I had no feeling in my face or my hands.

He radioed Jo-burg requesting an emergency descent. Once we were at an altitude where the oxygen levels in the cockpit were restored, my composure returned. Upon inspection, we found there were cracks in the tubing to my oxygen mask. We investigated further and found that all the tubing to the five passengers had cracks from years of limited use and the extreme temperatures in the African bush. The harsh climate took a toll on everything.

Fortunately, Dad's remained functional. God was with us that day. The outcome could have been tragic if both of us had become oxygen-deprived. The condition remains an all-too-common cause of catastrophe — the stupor and coma from high-altitude hypoxia, where oxygen levels drop, creeps on unexpectedly and results in death. After that incident, double-checking oxygen masks became a standard on the pre-flight check list.

Dad referred to me as his "precocious child" (Mum called me "doll baby" or "princess"). As a preschooler, before we moved to Africa, I went with him on numerous trips. On a flight to Seattle in the Cessna 172, we were placed in a holding pattern because of commercial traffic and the typical "socked in" Seattle weather on the ground — not the best flight circumstances. Having the added responsibility of a young daughter to care for increased the tenseness of the situation. All I knew was my daddy was preoccupied and we were flying in circles for what seemed like eternity.

"Are we in China yet?" I asked.

He grinned. "Almost."

I am sufficiently vertically challenged that I can't see directly forward out the front windshield, so I wasn't able to see the horizon or the ground below. I learned to fly purely by reading the plane's instruments. Dad said he used to watch me peering through the yoke when I was little, just to scan the panel.

HOTDOGS for HYENAS

Years later, while in my last year of high school, a flight instructor in South Africa told him I'd done a champion job flying a Cessna 150 Aerobat. Only problem, the instructor said, was that I never looked outside, not once. I could fly by the indicators for altitude and turn and bank. I could maintain straight and level flight with the best of them, without the assurance of actually seeing the ground before me. It came in handy as I became a more proficient flier.

But I loved to fly, this despite a period after an accident when I was just 12. It was a year before I got back into a cockpit and even then, I resisted with all my might. However, by my 16th birthday, I was not taking a driver's license exam like most adolescents, but rather the written pilot's and radio operator's exams. The happiest day in my life was when my brother left for college—there would be no more squabbling about who was going to fly "first-seat." With him gone, I reveled in being the only child and got in as many hours as I desired.

During the flight home, I marveled again at the vastness of Africa and the pristine desolation. "Once Africa gets into your blood," they say, "you are never the same." Now happy tears were streaming down my face.

I turned my head towards the window and bit my bottom lip so my parents would not see how emotional this was for me. As we flew home, I mentioned to Dad that I'd been flipped on my back the last week of school and the doctor had put me on some medications. Matter of fact, the medication was so strong, I went to sleep at London's Heathrow airport, nearly missing my flight home.

"What's the name of the meds?" asked Dad.

I was clueless. "Something like Dee-law-oh-did."

He shook his head. "When we get home, give that crap to me and I'm going to throw it away." It was years later that I learned the doctor, whom I had seen only once, had given me Dilaudid for my back for the flight to Rhodesia. Dilaudid is equal in strength to Fentanyl. Suffice it to say that the current opioid epidemic has long and deep roots.

HOTDOGS FOR HYENAS

G.P. & S. 2142—3,000—30-1-61.   C.A. FORM 85.

I. ~~FEDERATION~~ OF RHODESIA A~~ND NYASALAND~~

II.   **STUDENT PILOT'S LICENCE**
            (Flying Machines)

III. Number of Licence   2602

IV. Name of holder, in full:

    Pamela Kay

    COURTNEY

V. Address of holder   P.O. Box 40,

    NUANETSI.

VI. Nationality of holder   American

VII. Signature of holder   *Pam Courtney*

19

HOTDOGS FOR HYENAS

As we began our descent to the landing pattern of the 2,000-foot runway (which included the overruns), I peered outside the window. I could see crooked cattle trails, the occasional *kraal* with the women cooking over an open fire, a herd of wildebeest mixed with their companion zebras heading towards the water, and the Nuanetsi River, the water source for our mission. I looked back at the smoke from the open cooking fire. I couldn't wait to breathe in the smell of the *mopani* tree smoke and have it saturate my clothes.

As we approached the mission, I wanted to see all the new buildings from the air, so we flew an extra lap around. This also gave me a chance to look at the cooking fires from the village at the end of the runway. Perfect. Into the wind.

I could see patients pouring out into the clinic courtyard, raising their hands above their heads in welcome. I banked in front of the 450-foot *kopje* (granite outcropping). The windsock my mother had expertly made agreed with the cooking fires. Spot on.

Kopjes dot the landscape of Zimbabwe.

"Don't have to worry about being pushed down the runway today," I said. Mum, who never wanted to learn to fly, was forever the cautious passenger, barely looked up from her needlework.

"I heard that," she said.

I came in a wee bit "hot" (too fast) so I cut back the throttle and flared over the fence at the end of the runway. We came to a stop just before the hangar and turned left onto the apron. Dad poked me. "Good landing, all three of them." There were always inside family jokes.

I looked back at Dad. "Well, you never have to accuse me of stretching the glide!"

If you come in hot and try to put the plane on the ground, it bounces and you become airborne again, getting a second chance to meet the ground with less than take-off speed. The key is to hit the ground just as the speed drops to less than lift-off levels. My third "landing" was a charm!

During the taxi to the hangar, I could see the school children running through the doors to the dusty school yard. They were dancing, spinning, jumping, singing in unison. The joy of these children cannot be captured in words.

The positive impact of my parents on the local population can't be minimized—the community was a little utopia. The school children rushed to the fence, with the headmaster trying to maintain some rapidly deteriorating decorum. They'd known I was coming home.

When I stepped onto the apron in front of the hangar, I waved at them. In unison, they said, "Good Morning, Missy Pa-may-la." Jimius, our most trusted all-round employee, and our gardener Amon, followed by one of our cantankerous dachshunds, anxiously waited to say hello. Mum was still grating over my hair color. At least the household help knew who I was and never mentioned my brunette locks or what kind of *muti* (medicine) I put on my hair. Amon said, "Missy Pa-may-la, you are *too, too* white. We did not know." I hadn't realized that two years in sunless Seattle would turn me into a white person.

It was then that I began to notice a difference in my parents' behavior. We had talked about terrorist activities on the flight home to the mission. "Always be aware of your surroundings" was one of Dad's cautions. But my parents weren't behaving in that manner.

I felt very uneasy. I could see that they had been living among the turmoil for so long that they were oblivious to signs I was aware of. "Why are you not carrying a weapon when you go to get the mail?" I asked.

"Oh, Pam," said Dad, "it's been really quiet of late."

HOTDOGS for HYENAS

My initial concerns were overrun by the joy that I was home. I could smell the dirt of Africa. I determined then and there I was going to surrender my U.S. passport and become a Rhodesian citizen.

But first, I needed some alone time. Seattle was a city of continuous sirens and noise. Until I had gone to university, I had never before lived in a city. The noise level in the heart of a city is generally so loud that you cannot hear your own heartbeat. I craved the noiseless peace desperately. A soothing calm permeated my soul.

Mum had been waiting for my arrival and a chance to feed me my favorite foods. She gave me *biltong* (Afrikaans for bulls' tongue, our dried "jerky"-like meat) on the flight back to the mission. It was *lekker* (delicious). Beef was cheap. A T-bone steak cost around 25 U.S. cents per pound.

All I wanted was *boerewors*—a coarse-cut sausage with coriander spice mixed in with pork, beef and a little lamb. Jimius knew exactly how to build the fire and how the embers should be to cook the meat just right. Just wood, no briquettes. Before I even arrived home, Jimius had already started the fire for the *braai*. The coals were glowing the same orange as an African sunset.

I helped Mum set the round chipped marble table within feet of the *braai*. I cranked up the blue and white-striped umbrella, matched by the chairs. My mouth was watering. The smell of the wors, as we called it, was wafting over to where I was placing the serviettes (napkins) under the forks and the dessert fork and spoon at the top of the plate in opposite directions. I always loved setting the table and pouring tea. There was something magical about pulling dinner together.

We sat down at the table. Dad, Mum and me. "Tomorrow, I'd like to ride over to see Bob and Denise," I said. Both Bob and Denise Gawker had a great hand in raising me. I couldn't wait to spend an evening with them. Dad, his mouth full of steak, acknowledged my request by shaking his head up and down.

I felt like my life was coming back together again. Living in the U.S. was quickly fading. Why would anyone want to leave this garden of Eden? We had it made. I loved my country. I loved the people. I loved the feel of it. I was home.

After dinner, I walked into my bedroom. Everything was exactly as I had left it two long years before. Mum had painstakingly maintained my space. My black and white op-art curtains with matching bedspread, my cream and gold French provincial furniture with matching dressing table and cream leather-topped stool, cream-colored tufted headboard, pink sheets, *David Copperfield* and *The Prince and the Pauper* on the bookcase, abstract art I had painted in high school.

I opened my 9-foot-long closet. Crafted with a young woman in mind, my dad hand-built a shoe rack in the middle with rods for hanging clothes on either side. Mum had painted the half-round trim to match the shelves above my desk. But there was more to this space. The entire back of my closet was a stepped-in horizontal closet with a wood lid. Inside it contained the batteries to run lights for our bedsides after the generator was turned off nightly at 9 p.m. This allowed us to read books in bed. But the closet was also designed for protection. In case of a terrorist attack, it was another place to drop into for safety, undetected.

Nothing had been touched. I went to the lounge and slid an album onto the turntable, walked into the bathroom and turned the faucet. Charlie, our angularly built gardener, who always wore a reed-woven Chinese coolie type hat and sandals made of bicycle tires, had built a roaring fire in the outdoor hot water system (known as a donkey) before he left for the day. Hot water tumbled into the tub.

After years of rough bush living, we had a bathroom fit for royalty. I thought back to taking Jimius to a house years before at the Free Methodist mission near the Lundi River. Still under construction, we wandered around the unfinished rooms until we came to the bathroom. I explained to him that the stubbed-in plumbing was where the family could stand and wash their hands. He nodded in affirmation. And in the next space the family could lay down and wash their body. He thought this was outstanding as well. Then I pointed to an empty spot where the toilet would be installed. "This is the place where you go outside," I said.

He was stunned. "Inside?" He thought this was totally insane and unsanitary that anyone would defecate inside the home where you ate, slept and bathed. Our tub was a luxurious six feet in length. The tub and matching pedestal sink were a vibrant pink. I'm sure the color scheme was to meet Mum's femininity because Dad was not a pink kind of guy and we were the only family in the Lowveld that didn't have white fixtures. The tub was encased in grey mottled tile that matched the walls. The toilet (PK) was in a separate room next door.

The door to the bathroom had a skeleton key; the walls were concrete block. In case of a terrorist attack that was one room we knew to go to for safety. Just climb into the cast iron tub. Above the tub was a small jalousie window that could be cranked open and shut. I remember wondering just how safe a room could be with a window.

But tonight, that was the least of my concerns. I lay back in the tub, dribbled a washcloth over my exposed chest and listened to Simon and Garfunkel crank out "The Boxer" followed by "Cecilia."

I had lost count of the number of nights I'd emerged from that tub, soaking wet, and climbed into bed during the hottest months (beginning in October). There was no ick factor of getting sheets or bedding wet. It dried in minutes and I was able to get a good night sleep. When I was little, our nearest neighbor, Denise Gawler, a seasoned rancher's wife in her early twenties, who kept her nails polished beautifully and made smoking look like an elegant necessity of life, introduced me to this type of body cooling. With the last round of "Cecilia, you're breaking my heart, you're breaking my confidence daily," I reached up to grab a towel that had been dried from the arid heat on the outside clothesline. The familiar scratchiness of the sun-dried terrycloth felt wonderful. I inhaled the fragrance of the towel. The sun had baked in the freshness I had craved during my absence.

I told my parents I was going to sleep outside that night. I took a sleeping bag and two dachshunds, Madchen and Charge, and headed for the apron outside the hangar. I shook the torch (flashlight) a couple of times to make sure it was at its brightest—I'd nearly stepped on a puff adder a time or two on the rock sidewalk at night. Snakes so lazy they won't get out of the way, inviting anyone to raise their ire and inflict with a poisonous bite.

Once I spread out the sleeping bag and crawled in, the dogs dove to the bottom. Dachshunds love to burrow. It is a natural tendency. I'd missed these long lean black and tan "hot dogs" who would wriggle into giant 8-foot-high ant hills and then back out unhappily while being reprimanded that they could be a python's next meal.

I gasped as I gazed at the gallery of the Southern night sky for the first time in two years. The stars seemed so close and clear they appeared within touch. I rolled over to my left and scanned the sky. Yes, there was the Southern Cross. I had always been fascinated with the stars and cosmos. When Jimius had asked me to name his first child, I selected "Stella" (Latin for star). *Oh, yeah*, I thought, *I'm going to have to drive to his village and see Stella tomorrow.*

Now, in the absolute stillness of the night, the occasional shooting star would streak by and then disappear. I attended a spectacular performance—all I had to do was lie there and breathe. We pay hundreds of dollars to be entertained, take weekend trips to have our souls refreshed, pay yoga instructors to help us get our bodies in tune, or enter houses of worship for one hour of spiritual uplifting. Yet I had it all at my fingertips. I stared straight up at the pristine African nocturnal cosmos and could feel the primal power of my heartbeat—I was right in the middle of the Creator's craftsmanship. Soon, my mind drifted into the magical world of slumber.

It would be short-lived. "Pam, Pam, wake up. You need to come to the house right now!" Still on my back, I opened my eyes and saw the outline of my mother's face inches from my nose. "Why?" I asked.

Mum said, "We were woken up by sounds."

I didn't ask *what* sounds. I only wanted to close my eyes and go back to sleep. I was exhausted and sleep-deprived from the grueling 25-hour flight. I had dreamed of this night frequently during the intervening two years and I was a bit irritated. I had become unaccustomed to parental controls.

But I knew well enough to heed when Mum warned. My instincts of bush upbringing kicked in. We were all responsible for each other; not listening could cost you your life and that of others around you. So, I crawled out of the sleeping bag with the blue-flannel-striped lining — an item my parents purchased shortly after they married. They had purchased two sleeping bags and zipped them together. During their early married years, they had a Harley, a pup tent and the sleeping bags, all of which had weathered more than a few storms. I scooped up the two black and tan dachshunds, and with an arm around each one, reluctantly followed Mum past the hangar and onto the rough granite walkways to the house. The slabs of granite had been chipped away from a nearby *kopje*, loaded in the back of our Dodge Power Wagon and brought back to the mission. All our sidewalks, garden and fountain walls and decking around the pool look just like this. Granite joined with cement bonds. Very artistic, but very common in this part of Africa. Even though the moonlight was like sunlight, I still looked down. No puff adders tonight. Once inside, I crawled into my luxurious bed. My sleep was again disturbed. It only seemed like minutes had passed, but it was daylight. "Come quick," Mum said. "Go see where you were sleeping last night."

I slipped on my flip-flops and ran down the hall and out the side door. I could hear Jimius, Amon, and Charlie, clucking in Shona mixed with English. "Eh, Eh, Eh, Ma Wei. Ag, this is a very (with a large rolling accent on the "r") very (he made even more dramatic) grave situation."

I smiled to myself. I'd missed these three. They were sometimes over the top in their fears. Then I heard Jimius say, "Missy Pa-may-la has slept with these creatures." His rolling of the first "r" in creature made it seem even more ominous.

We all stood in horror as we looked at where my sleeping bag had been spread. By now, my dogs had followed me to the spot and begun their customary sniffing.

HOTDOGS FOR HYENAS

The noise my parents had heard was the "laughter" of hyenas. The visible tracks, the *spoor*, the smell of their urination, all hyena.

I immediately felt nauseous. They had been attracted to the smell of the dachshunds—little dogs are high on hyenas' savory snack list. Hyenas are savage with iron clad jaws.

What teeth you have, Mr. Hyena!

They shred. They rip. They are ruthless. They belong to a matrilineal society with females raging three times the amount of testosterone as their male counterparts. A pack of hyenas can devour an entire zebra leaving no leftovers, not even the bones, in less than a half hour. Hemingway wrote of their disgusting behavior in *Green Hills of Africa (1935)*:

> *Fisi, the hyena,*
> *hermaphroditic self-eating*
> *devourer of the dead, trailer*
> *of calving cows, ham-*
> *stringer, potential biter-off*
> *of your face at night while*
> *you slept, say yowler, camp-*
> *follower, stinking, foul, with*
> *jaws that crack the bones*
> *the lion leaves, belly*
> *dragging, loping away on the*
> *brown plain...*

We had been spared. That night, at least, there had been no hot dogs for hyenas.

2
CHANGE FOREVER

Before returning to Africa in 1972, I made a serious decision to become a Rhodesian citizen. I'd had permanent residency there since our arrival years before. I was almost 20 years old and knew this was where I belonged.

I had had the experience of America as my parents requested. Now, I was making a commitment to the country where I had grown up. My father drove with me the 40 miles to the post office and police station at Nuanetsi. We checked our mailbox outside and then stood in line where I would surrender my U.S. passport.

I had pulled my passport out of its zebra skin case. It was smaller than British and Rhodesian passports and I was only too happy to have a passport that better fit my regionally-made case.

While we were standing there, Dad said, "You know Pam, that U.S. passport is your ticket out of here."

"What do you mean?" I asked.

"Things are going to get really hot here soon. The war is going to get extremely tough. If you surrender your American passport, you will have a difficult time finding a country that will take you as a Rhodesian."

That was the first time I'd heard him acknowledge that our bush war would likely spill over into something big, that many of us would be fleeing the country.

HOTDOGS for HYENAS

"I know you want to go to university in South Africa," he continued. "Let's look into that, but the traveling back and forth may not be safe either. I'd like for you to go to Europe for a while — just a bit, not long. When the war is over you can come back home."

None of this really made sense to me. People were going to flee, but then come home? I knew right then that Dad knew more than he was letting on. I'd been concerned that my parents had developed a cavalier attitude about safety issues that had been part of our daily routine. I couldn't make out whether they were so close to the situation that they didn't take precautions, or if they were trying to not worry me about farm attacks that were getting closer to home. I realized then that it was the latter. They hadn't anticipated that I would return with a decision to no longer be an American.

Within days of being home, I had already learned who had had "near misses," had run over landmines, or who had not survived farm attacks.

One of our neighbors had a nightly ritual that had resulted in a broken toe. Their master bedroom was on the second floor, with an outside balcony that caught the nighttime breezes. He slept with a string tied around his toe and the night watchman, who was trusted and had been with him for years, was responsible for waking the family up if terrorists had slipped through the gate. A tug on the string was the silent warning to get up. And it worked, until the night watchman, in a panic, *jerked* on the string attached to my neighbor's toe. Cr-a-a-a-a-ck.

We had big barking guard dogs, too. For years, my mum had a rule that had been instilled since she'd learned of the pitfalls of Europeans during the Mau Mau uprising in Kenya. She cooked the food, *sadza* and mince (hamburger) for the dogs every day and *she* fed them.

We didn't have "Kibbles and Bits" back then. Our dogs ate fresh every day. It would have been so easy to have the house boy or someone else feed them, but Mum trained our dogs to take food *only* from family members. Ground glass or poisons often led to many

CHANGE FOREVER

farm dogs being coaxed into eternal silence, allowing a raid on the farm or mission occupants to take place. We learned that even if the dogs barked at night not to step out with the porch light on. The illumination made you a vulnerable target in a terrorist attack.

Our family home was U-shaped. In the middle was a fenced and terraced back yard with a serpentine-type curb separating the levels. Directly from the lounge (living room), a glass door led out to a stamped concrete patio that filled up the space from wall to wall and built-in planters for Mum's exotic plants. The second level of the back yard was grass and at one corner a huge *braai* (concrete grill) was in continual use.

After my return, other than working at the clinic, I had little responsibility for a few months. With family and friends, we took off to a favorite game watering hole at Gonarezhou National Park.

The elephants of Gonarezhou are dwarfed by the Chilojo Cliffs—a favorite place.

HOTDOGS FOR HYENAS

The first night we slept on an old low-lying concrete bridge. Hidden by brush, the nighttime grazing elephants came within feet of where we were stretched out. The next night, we dragged a mattress high up in the crotch of a tree. As we laid in this amazing cradle, game animals, segregated by species, came to get their nighttime drinks. First came the impala and kudu, followed by warthogs, zebra, wildebeest, giraffes and finally elephants and buffaloes. Around 3 a.m. the big cats began to roar.

How could anyone take this magical universe for granted?

I was starved for sunshine after sunless Seattle so my new daily ritual included "laying out" to get some color back in my skin. On one such afternoon, I heard a noise on the reed fence that surrounded the back yard and pool and rolled over on my back. I squinted — even through my sunglasses, the rays were harsh.

Resting on top of the six-foot fence was one of the largest leguaans (lizard) I'd ever seen. It must have been close to five feet long. I was surprised the dogs hadn't gone crazy over the disturbance of this humongous and very unwelcome visitor.

I slid off the lounge chair and walked into the living area of our home and quietly padded past the fireplace, took a left at the hall, and went straight into my parents' bedroom. The gun safe was built into the wall just past their bedroom door. I unlocked the heavy steel door with a skeleton key and tugged it open, reaching for the Colt .45 that was resting in a holster on a low shelf between two shotguns. I slid the .45 out of the holster and closed the door with my hip.

With the gun in hand, I stepped back out on the patio. The leguaan was still there, its tongue darting in and out.

"Ugh, *Jy is lelik* (you are ugly)," I said in Afrikaans. I sat down on the lounge chair with the gun still in my hand, watching the leguaan move slowly down the fence.

OK, I thought, we can't have that thing creeping around. So, I leveled the .45 at the giant lizard and pulled the trigger. **Thunk.** It bounced off rocks into a small freshly painted pond, fed by a fountain.

I loved dangling my feet in the shallow pool with the marine

CHANGE FOREVER

blue painted interior. The area around the pond was built with rough granite and cantilevered at the edge, a super-nice addition my brother designed and built. He'd found the loose pieces of rock at a nearby *kopje*, and let nature take its course. The water from the pump flowed down the natural rock impressions into the pond. From there, he created a fountain that sent water up in an arch to the pond.

I walked back to my chaise lounge, pulled out my book, and went back to reading and listening to '70s rock music on LM radio — broadcast from Lorenzo Marques, Mozambique. We had all grown up listening to American D.J. Casey Kasum count down the top 20 hits every week since the mid-60s.

Charlie, ever the brave one, immediately yelled for everyone to come look at the lizard. I heard the back door open and close and Dad poked his head out.

"Is everything okay? I heard a gunshot," he said.

I pointed towards the now very dead leguaan. Dad always had a couple of dogs that followed him everywhere. They squeezed around him to see what the excitement was about. The first one to the lizard claimed it, growling.

Xhoco, I clicked to the dog. "Get away." Followed by *buya lapa* in the Ndebele language — "come here." The little dachshund reluctantly came to me, sad that her trophy was being carted off by Charlie.

The British South Africa Police (BSAP) conducted three week patrols out in our area, collecting information about terrorist activities and movement. One patrol officer, Tom, had been my friend for several years — we'd been tennis partners during the years he was assigned to his post at Nuanetsi. He stopped by often to be fed by my mum during the patrols. It was perfectly legal for him to dine with the family, but he wasn't allowed to sleep in our home, so after dinner, he would gather his gear into his Land Rover and head out another 30 miles through the bush to set up camp.

Every Friday, I would drive 40 miles to get the mail at Nuanetsi, and then drive on to Rutanga to buy meat or pick up supplies Dad had shipped through the railway. On one of Tom's rounds, Dad stopped him. "Pam wants to go pick up the mail, stay for tennis and a *braai*," he said. "Would you accompany her?"

Tom, who was around 21 and had a face full of acne, felt honored that Dad trusted him to take care of me. He left his Land Rover and his automatic weapon with my parents and we took my weapon and the family vehicle. As was customary, we told my parents that we would be back at 11:00 p.m. And that's what we meant—punctuality was key. Not home at 11:02? A search party would come looking.

I put the Land Rover in reverse and backed away from the house. Hmm, I thought, my weapon, my Land Rover, me driving. Who is babysitting whom? Then I realized that Dad would rather have me behind the wheel with someone else covering me because I knew the roads and shortcuts like the back of my hand.

I slipped the Landy into 4-wheel drive as I approached the steep incline into the first riverbed. We headed towards Greenspan's Ranch (owned by two brothers who lived in Bulawayo), where we would bisect its 10,000 acres, traveling through nine gates and nine cattle crossings. Once across, we were another riverbed away from the tarmac that led to the police station, but once we crossed the bridge, we made a right onto two miles of teeth-jarring, dust-enveloping roads.

Once our tennis, swimming, and partying were over, we headed back through the bush. There was no moon in sight.

About six miles into Greenspan's, Tom said, "I forgot my ammo."

I stared at him in the darkness. I had a decision to make—turn Tom loose without ammo or take on my parents for being late. "You can't go back on patrol for three weeks with no ammo. We need to turn around."

The fastest we could drive on the bush road was between 35 and 40 mph; we were flying. I slid into the police station, Tom jumped out, and minutes later, he emerged with boxes and bandoliers.

"Right," I said, "let's get moving." I drove as fast as I could.

When we pulled into the driveway, the house was as dark as ink—only recognizable by its outline. There was not even a flashlight on. Mum was standing in the kitchen, fully clothed.

CHANGE FOREVER

"Sorry, Mrs. Courtney," Tom said. "I forgot all my ammo. I have to get back on patrol."

I stood at the door of my parents' bedroom while Mum opened the safe and handed Tom his weapon. Normally, she would have told him he was welcome to sleep at the house, knowing he would decline. Tonight she didn't extend that invitation. Dad, who was in the bedroom, never even wished him good luck on the patrol.

I shuffled down to my bedroom and pulled back the covers on my bed. Dad was there within seconds.

"So, what exactly were the two of you doing?"

I repeated what had happened and where I had turned around. He wasn't buying the story. I wanted to say, "Dad, Tom is not my type," but that's not the kind of conversation I would have ever dreamed of having with my dad. Besides, I think he genuinely knew that I wasn't interested in Tom in that way. So, I looked up at Dad's six-foot frame and said, "The weather is dry, and my tire tracks will show you exactly where I turned around. I'll be more than happy to show you in the morning and then onto Nuanetsi where you can verify the checkout log for ammo." It was the first time I stood toe-to-toe with my dad.

Years later he told me that he had watched me choose my battles and know when to stand on principle. "It was difficult to swallow my pride and admit my little girl had grown up," he said.

With that incident over, we settled back into our normal routines in the bush. My mother had one episode of being "bush happy" (equivalent to cabin fever). I'd heard stories growing up of people getting bush happy and having to be taken into town to be cared for, but never dreamed of my mum having this affliction.

Never. Mum was stoic. She was a rock. She handled my dad's somewhat roller coaster behavior with expertise. Dad was quoted once as having said he and Mum were blessed with children who never complained, even under the harshest conditions. I was blessed with having a mother who also never complained. She thanked God for every lesson she learned. She committed herself to her own daily devotional time.

So, when I saw her emotionally dissolving before my very eyes, I never asked why. I didn't discuss it with Dad. I solved it by loading her up and driving her 50 miles to the nearest hotel, The Lion & Elephant. I ordered her a glass of red wine, which she maybe took two sips of. I took her hand for a brief moment. "Mum," I said, "do you need to get out of the bush for a while? Go to town? Go to South Africa? Does Dad really know how hard you work?"

Mum and I had never developed a girly-girl, let's-go-shopping relationship. But at that moment, she let her guard down. "Do you think anyone at this bar will notice if I get a little tipsy?" I looked around the room. There was the bartender, local ranchers, a few travelers. We knew them all. Everyone understood. Everyone had a story.

I shook my head. "No one will care, Mum."

I could see she was feeling slightly uncomfortable with our openness, so I shifted gears. "Remember, the night when I met Ian Smith here? Let's talk about happy times." Smith, our prime minister, had joined us for a party with his entourage one evening. I was 16 and walked over to have a chat with him at his table. Ever so kind to everyone he met, he stood up from the table and invited me to join him and his staff. We talked about his farm and cattle and how much he loved farming.

Prime Minister Ian Smith required little security and was often seen riding his bike to work.

He was the leader of our country, but he did not stand on ceremony. During dinner he said to me, "My son would really like you."

CHANGE FOREVER

Mum and I finished our lighthearted chat, stood up from the table and wished everyone at the bar good night. I laid the rifle between us on the seat and drove Mum home that night. Not a word was spoken all the way home. We never talked about the high anxiety of bush living and the immense toll it was taking on us, because this was our new normal. We were fiercely self-reliant, both physically and emotionally.

As I said before, I went to the clinic every day to work with Dad. It took me a couple days to get reaccustomed to medical horrors that previously I'd taken in stride. I could feel my stomach roll as I looked at fresh burns on small children. "Come on, Pam, I'd say to myself, this shouldn't bother you at all."

My absence had softened me or had made me more sensitive, to say the least. The night before I was to depart Africa for Europe, a set of twins had been born at the clinic. I wasn't present for the delivery, but heard they were premature.

As the sun came up, I ran to the clinic to see them. I rushed through the front door and asked where they were. One of the nursing students I didn't know well reported they had both quit breathing shortly after delivery and died.

I asked what she had done with the babies. She said she wrapped them in a towel and put them in the x-ray room. I ran through the surgery room and into x-ray. I tore back the towel—both babies were dusky, but breathing. Their little hearts were beating! I yelled for help. I took my jacket off and wrapped it around the towel that was holding these precious lives and ran to the phone that connected the clinic to the house.

Dad answered and told me he had been informed that the twins had expired. I asked for a roll of aluminum foil, which I wrapped around them for further insulation, and added a hot water bottle. I ran with the babies across the airfield to the hangar and Dad already had the aircraft rolled out. I jumped in with the babies in my arms.

We landed at the Swedish hospital 25 minutes after takeoff. The staff was waiting and whisked these tiny survivors to the hospital.

I returned to the mission and finished packing. Once again, I was leaving Africa, my life, my heart, and our family home.

We all thought I'd be coming back soon. But we were wrong. Our home would be turned into rubble. Terrorists turned our illusion of security into a jumble of grey cinder blocks. A cannon had been turned on our front yard by "freedom fighters." The terraced back yard was destroyed, the pool filled with dirt.

What most of you reading this won't understand is that it took months of preparation and patience to build our home. Everything was carefully orchestrated. Timber for the roof trusses had to be shipped in from Canada (ample supply of trees and no embargo). To get a single window frame trucked in and to have the glass for the windows and doors arrive without being shattered required intricate planning. Our roofs were constructed of asbestos instead of tin — another lesson learned from watching other countries combating terrorists' petrol bombs.

But at the end of the war, our home would have but one wall still standing. Poignantly, it was the wall of my bedroom, instantly recognizable because it was painted a school bus yellow.

Our home finally destroyed by terrorists.

CHANGE FOREVER

Consequently, a yellow wall and chunks of concrete would be the last vestiges of my childhood home.

The Rhodesian bush war impacted everyone who lived and loved this extraordinary country. Utopia to rubble, and for what? The black-white and black-black power struggles there decimated all vestiges of civilization. A pristine environment was demolished in the misplaced name of freedom, a government removed and replaced with anarchy and genocide—no bargain in anyone's mind. But, for me, it was personal. It was all I knew of "home."

With the firing of one artillery shell, only our memories remained.

PART 2

3
THE BIG MOVE

When we hear that someone has been called to serve, it's normal that we let it go right there. We rarely ask, "How did it happen? Was there a burning bush?"

Deep inside, I think most of us would concur that we're happy that it's someone else, not us, that's being called. I was the catalyst for my family's decision to move to Africa. My parents had received invitations to other mission fields in China and Japan but turned those down. The call to Africa was more urgent.

I was born in 1952, quite healthy initially. But soon it was clear that a devastating calamity was emerging. The diagnosis: erythroblastosis, a disease wherein a healthy newborn's blood is destroyed through an allergic reaction from blood coming from the mother during labor. All the healthy oxygen-carrying red blood cells are ripped apart, spilling the bilirubin and iron into the serum far too rapidly for the tiny baby to digest and handle. The torn red cells reduce the oxygen-carrying capability reflected as anemia. The yellow jaundice is severe. Often the kidneys fail from the onslaught of toxins overwhelming the baby's limited filtering capacity.

Few "blue babies" survived in that era. The outlook was not good for me. My parents had dreamed of having a large family—they wanted seven kids—but were advised against having more children. It was common knowledge that these allergic reactions worsened with each subsequent pregnancy. They were told the next child would definitely not survive.

Today we prevent this condition with proaction. If the mother and the father have incompatible blood types, the mother receives a shot to prevent her producing antibodies to the baby's blood.

The condition never occurs with the first pregnancy. A scant amount of the first baby's blood enters the mother's bloodstream during labor and acts to introduce foreign proteins, causing the production of antibodies that cause no problems—until the delivery of a subsequent child with the same offending blood type. I was the unlucky victim of a disease that has since been eliminated.

I was in serious condition. I received multiple blood transfusions, exhausting my IV sites. Veins collapsed, necessitating a "cutdown" to surgically find a vessel able to accept the life's blood and left me with an unsightly scar on my leg, just above my ankle.

Mother stood in the nursery next to my cot praying, "God, we've had her for only a short time. If you have to take her, she's yours." What she didn't know was that my dad, who was working on the surgical staff in the hospital, was standing at the doorway listening to her prayer. He privately prayed that if God spared my life, he would serve wherever he was called.

An innovative research protocol was identified, the rare blood exchange was ordered and miraculously performed. They removed the toxic blood and replaced it with healthy blood in a matter of hours. I not only survived, but thrived.

I grew up in a home with a strong spiritual presence. My parents never made a decision without committing to prayer. They never went to bed at night without recounting and acknowledging the blessings of the day. They served in their church tirelessly. Before moving to Africa, our Sunday mornings and evenings and Wednesday evenings were filled with church events.

My brother and I were not always enthusiastic participants. Mum would keep me still with a half stick of gum or a nap on her lap. My brother, who had a watch with a second hand, would count

THE BIG MOVE

how long some long-winded prayer lasted. But all in all, we were good, obedient kids. Our nuclear family was strong. Our values were deeply rooted.

Dad maintained that we were happy and content with our lives. "We had everything we had dreamed of," he often said. "We had accomplished the educational goals we had set, and our careers were evolving as planned. We were strong supporters of missionaries, and several missionaries even came to visit us at the church in Oregon—many of whom were excellent speakers."

One of them, Max Ward Randall, left a particularly favorable impression. He had opened new fields in Africa, was a bush pilot, and had authored several books about his experience. Max was equally impressed with my parents and sent them a letter—his mission group had been offered a new area in Southern Rhodesia and if they could find someone to come who could fulfill the government's significant prerequisites, it would be a godsend.

Max asked if we would come. "It only took about five minutes to answer," said my father. "We said no. We couldn't come. We didn't want to come. We were happy. It would be too disruptive to a fragile young family at this juncture."

During this period, all correspondence between Africa and America took several weeks roundtrip. Several months later, another letter from Max arrived. "Would you at least pray about it?"

The mission still had not found anyone. They needed someone who had a unique blend of professional credentials as well as manual and outdoor survival skills. Following that letter, a cablegram arrived with the same urgent message. "Will you honestly pray about this matter?"

At that point, my parents opened their Bible and reviewed Acts 13 to give God a chance to speak. The emotional and intellectual ice began to thaw. Dad sent a cablegram back agreeing to pray. "We did understand what we were being called to do," he said. "That was to bring the Gospel and salvation to a people that had never heard of Jesus. We were to bring medical treatment to people that had never been treated by Western medicine. We were going to educate African children where they had no concept of what a school was. We were committed to bringing hope where there was no hope."

While I do not remember the incident at the tender age of five, my parents sat down with my older brother, Michael, and me and said, "This is what we've been offered. Here are the needs, wants, and challenges. There are no schools. No hospitals. No place to live." They spelled out very graphically that life would not be easy. This opportunity would be very primitive, and they would have only the basic necessities to survive. Dad said he did not sway us by saying this was something Daddy wanted to do. Every member of the family had a vote, he would explain later, and it would have to be 100 percent for us to consider going. Everyone had plenty of opportunity to say, "I don't think so" or "I don't know" or "I'm afraid."

In the end, there was a united decision within the family that yes, we would do this. We understood this would be a call from God, and it wouldn't be an easy one. In a logical sense, this decision came up empty and dubious, but in a spiritual sense, we all felt the power of God in our lives and the faith that the Lord would keep and protect us.

Following the decision and announcement, we began packing up to leave for the bush. My parents created a mission advisory board to discuss the projected monthly budget we would need to build and then maintain this new foothold in Africa.

When the board sat down for the first time, they found the task extremely difficult, because there were no facts on which to base the estimates. The primitive region to which we were going had not been penetrated by Westerners, so there were no yardsticks to compare.

Dad knew he would have to establish a reliable water source. He knew he would have to build buildings, even making his own bricks and blocks. He knew he would have to hire a labor force of local Africans. As he defined every conceivable project, the list grew longer. He calculated the cost of building a school to house a hundred students would be $2,800. He continued to itemize the costs of building and operating a clinic, including equipment and maintenance. The list expanded. He soon arrived at a sound baseline figure of $1,000 per month, which he called a "service link." Dad consulted several missionaries to establish an estimate of his family's personal cost of living, which included insurance, pension, food, fuel, clothing, and education. He concluded his family would need $400 per month, and he called this stipend a "living link."

The final step before going out to raise funds was to secure a forwarding agent. All committed funds would be sent to the forwarding agent, who would then disperse a monthly check to us. Dad said, "Among the hundreds of people needed to keep missionaries on the field, none is more important than the forwarding agent."

Almost immediately his speaking schedule was filled. He began speaking to churches and organizations. He presented his personal journey and vision eloquently and convincingly, replete with slides of Africa. The need to evangelize Africa became a cross not just for my family, but also for those who could not make the personal journey with us. They could at least help financially. Soon commitments for the necessary $1,400 per month were pledged.

"In the final analysis," Dad would say, "the true tests of a mission's worth are the advances made for the Kingdom of God." He estimated that the cost of converting a single African to Christianity was approximately $70. That is, every $70 spent on the entire mission program (personal living expenses included), would result in one new baptism. "An interesting comparison could be made Stateside, where the average cost per convert was $7,000. With this in mind, we were able to say that the investment in Africa was a wise one."

Several critical purchases needed to be made before we could leave for the mission field. After careful investigation, and upon receiving recommendations from the field, my parents purchased a Dodge 300 Power Wagon, with four-wheel drive and a winch, for $4,500. The one-ton truck was equipped with a Perkins (British-manufactured) diesel engine. The diesel engine was ordered to offset the high fuel costs in Africa. It was common for missionaries to drive 20,000 miles per year. Gasoline was seventy-five cents per gallon as opposed to twenty-three cents for diesel. The difference in fuel cost was sufficient to justify considerable the installation of the diesel power plant.

Next my parents ordered an expansive flatbed for the Dodge truck's chassis. This would allow Dad to carry the types of loads he knew he would have to transport through the bush. He intended to weld heavy-duty steel panels for sideboards once we arrived in Africa, allowing him to transport sand and rock for construction projects.

To fill the space on the back of the truck, he began in earnest designing and building a camper shell that could slide on and off as needed. He welded the frame with the help of a church member and then began the process of building a tiny camper dwelling that would have adequate storage space. He designed and built four jacks so the camper could also function freestanding. The truck, camper, and jacks were shipped by freighter to Cape Town, South Africa.

"When we got to the bush, we struggled," said Dad. "Once there, I knew I would never again get a truck like the one we had shipped over. It was a beautiful truck, and it had a lot of capabilities, but we couldn't drive on remote trails with it. It was too heavy, and the wide mirrors were not an asset but an impediment. We purchased the truck through the council of missionaries in Africa. They should have known that, where we were headed, this was not a proper vehicle."

Dad was an avid hunter (and Mum was skilled with a rifle). He knew that he would have to provide for the majority of the family's meat supply. In addition, weapons would be needed for protection against venomous snakes and wild animals. So before shipment of the camper, he secured a Winchester .30-30 and .375 (elephant gun), a Browning .458, an assortment of shotguns, and several handguns.

None of us understood the true sacrifices we were soon to make. Once the decision to go was final, Dad and Mum knew they might never see their parents again, a sobering notion. But before Mum was even confronted with that thought, she had to face the emotional task of parting with household furnishings. Many of these items held

THE BIG MOVE

special memories, having been purchased during the earlier, lean times of their marriage.

She could not fathom there would be no more family gatherings with the table leaves gently put in place and a starched tablecloth spread across the top. Family birthday parties and Christmas dinners with the grandparents would be a thing of the past. This was a deliberate death of the closely-knit family structure they had carefully nurtured.

This monumental move took place before the days of Saturday yard sales and the convenience of public storage. And it was confusing to my brother and me to have strangers walking through the house, peering inside Mum's prized china cabinet and running their hands over the matching Duncan Phyfe table.

She had saved all the knitted baby items and gowns she had made for us, assuming she would pass those on to future generations. She fought back tears as the nursery staff at the church took the baby clothes off her hands. The hardest decision was what to do with the family dog, a red dachshund named Shorty. At first, they considered taking her to Africa, but realized this would not be practical. Mum had to explain to me that Shorty would have to go to another loving family.

Mum simply could not part with her china and crystal and asked one of the grandmothers to box up those items and store them in the basement. The family violin, played by me at the age of three, found a home with the grandmother, too. Mum simply didn't have the will to let this heirloom go to a stranger.

The only films about Africa we had ever seen were black and white Tarzan movies. What an adventure, swinging through trees, living in a dense jungle, with chimps for friends!

"It was incredibly difficult to grasp what we were to embark upon," said Dad. He knew he was putting his entire family in a precarious situation, but preaching the Gospel, teaching the people, and ministering to their physical and spiritual needs far outweighed any self-focused negative thoughts. My very survival had been a miracle, and a sign that God had plans for my family. Dad reflected:

"In America, we took going to church for granted, never a privilege. Our children were spoon-fed in Sunday school; they were not hungry to hear Bible stories for the first time. As adults, we were too sophisticated to discuss the marvel of Jesus's conception, birth, baptism, and resurrection, never wondering what it would be like to hear it and have hope for the very first time. This is why we answered the call. I answered the call to evangelize a tiny portion of Africa. I immersed myself in the Scripture. I believed that no one should have the opportunity to hear the Gospel twice when there were people that had never heard it the first time. I knew I was a believer; therefore, I was a disciple, no different than the first twelve disciples that followed Jesus. There is no differentiation between us regardless of our socioeconomic levels. There are no first-class Christians or second-class Christians. I could not justify why I was entitled to stay in a comfort zone in America. I could not put a higher value on my or my family's life than someone who had less education than me but had a burning passion to share the Word. I was blessed with opportunities all of my life. I read and reread the Great Commission: 'Go into all the world and preach the Gospel to all creation' (Mark 16:15). We were being called."

While still in America, Dad immersed himself in the experiences of medical missionaries who had gone before him, including luminaries such as Moffat, Livingston and Schweitzer. He reread Dr. Albert Schweitzer until he knew some of the passages by memory. As he prayerfully considered his mission options in 1955, he said, "Dr. Schweitzer's voice spoke to my soul. Through his writings, I felt I had the strength and wisdom to embark on this journey into Africa."

Dr. Schweitzer was known as an *oganga*, or fetishman, by the Africans. The Africans had no name for doctor other than the one who practices the art of healing. Schweitzer's patients came to the logical conclusion that a man who could heal a disease had the same power to produce it, even at a distance! Schweitzer, who placed himself in the category of good healer, realized he was also in another category:

THE BIG MOVE

dangerous men. He came to understand that Africans believed that diseases came about not by a natural cause but through evil spirits, malicious human magic, or worms that invaded the body. He also realized that the medicine men employed poison to maintain their positions of authority. That, compounded with the indigenous people's fear of supernatural powers that one man can have over another, made Dr. Schweitzer realize he had a simple responsibility to bring a new and different perspective of the world that would free the Africans of these terrible superstitions.

He also spent a tremendous amount of time explaining, with the help of an experienced interpreter, how medicines were to be taken. He made the Africans repeat these directions over and over. In the end, he still wasn't sure whether the patients consumed the medications as directed or all at one time. My father was "moved by the honesty of Dr. Schweitzer. I realized," he said, "that I might be encountering some of the very same challenges that Schweitzer faced forty years previously."

And he was correct. Years later, when birth control pills became available, even though explained at the clinic in the Shona language, there was a challenge in ensuring that the women understood. On many occasions one might find women taking an entire month's supply of birth control pills at one time. What benefit was it to string the process out for an entire month when the course could be consumed at one gulp?

When the time came for us to leave, the good-byes were painful and nearly surreal. I remember seeing my parents cry for the first time. The tears flowed, but no one realized how final those good-byes would be.

The immediate and extended family gathered on the lawn of Mum's family home to see us off. I remember the grass being very damp and the cold seeping through my shoes. I looked up at all the faces trying to figure out why everyone was so sad. At my young age, I didn't grasp we were not going on a holiday, soon to return after a two-week trip.

My parents were introducing us to a new life and abandoning creature comforts and the routine of being a normal American family. But they believed that this wasn't merely a change in scenery but a true commitment, a commitment to being a positive role model for us and the new flock they were going to minister to.

Once we boarded the ship to Cape Town, we met an Afrikaans-speaking couple, the Van Zyls from South Africa. They were intimately familiar with our assigned destination and were astonished that an American family had committed to living in one of the harshest areas of the remote bush.

The husband, Piet, was full of questions. "What is your background for going into this area?"

"I have a background in medicine, ministry, and education," answered Dad.

"No, you have a minus, a zero and a plus for going there. Basically, you have precious little. Have you ever been there before?"

"No."

"And you're going there to do what?"

"Open up a new mission station in the bush."

"Do you speak the language?"

"No."

Every day the Van Zyls shook their heads in disbelief that our entire family was going into the area alone. For two weeks, they gave us our best introduction and education for living in the bush.

Upon landing in Cape Town, we cleared the truck through Customs. My family was ready, we thought, for the challenge put before us. How naïve. Having a pure heart was insufficient. Nothing in my parents' development prepared them for the evil emanating from others "of faith," in their jealousy and insincerity, who fought vigorously to destroy not just Dad, but our entire family.

Government authorities in Southern Rhodesia approved the use of a remote area in the south-central part of the country for a Christian mission. No whites had ever attempted to live there. Civilization had ignored this area. There was no electricity, no running water, no

THE BIG MOVE

plumbing or sanitation, no refrigeration, no communications, no air conditioning, no roads, and no radio or TV.

Sound like utopia? Not exactly. But this was where my family felt called to serve. No conceptual competition. Just innocent humans who had not yet heard the Word. The need to establish a mission that included churches, a clinic, and schools had been carefully researched for several years owing to the fact that this region had yet to be exposed to Christianity. The African population had occasionally seen a white male government official, but they had never seen a European woman or child. This area, known as the Lowveld, was frequently drought-stricken, with minimal rainfall. No Westerner had ever wanted to live there, let alone embark on the arduous task of carving out a permanent mission.

The potential new mission area was located in an African reserve called Maranda Tribal Trust Land. The land was government owned but assigned to the black Africans. The majority of the 10,000 Africans living there belonged to the Shona tribe. The tribal elders (*kraal* heads) voted for which denomination they wanted to settle in Maranda Tribal Trust Land. On closer examination, this particular protocol should have been a vibrant red warning flag; however, the need to serve was the overriding factor. How could there be a failure if we had faith? Remember, the old saying God never gives us more than we can handle.

My family accepted this challenge and moved 10,000 miles and five hundred years from the comforts of the United States to a primitive and desolate site named Melelzi. We arrived by ship from England in Cape Town, South Africa. We had shipped all the supplies, including the truck and slide—in a camper shell Dad had fabricated himself by hand, as part of the preparation in Oregon.

Paved roads carried us the first 1,400 miles to Fort Victoria, Rhodesia. We took numerous diversionary side jaunts to visit game parks and existing mission sites in an effort to acclimate the family.

But the efforts to calm jangled nerves were spoiled as the locals, both black and white colonialists, reacted in shock when we revealed our final destination. Even the Africans were dismayed that whites would consider such a venture. No matter who our God is, they said, there are limits to the risks we should assume, especially with a wife and two children. But Dad was unfazed.

The final 250 miles were treacherous, the last 100 far more difficult than we ever expected. The only navigation aid we had was a compass. There were no prior roads, no trails, and no guidance of any kind. Just hacking through the bush. This was well before iPhones and GPS. Machetes, axes, and winches helped us pull the truck through the bush. Because this was the rainy season, we had to ford streams. Hippos and crocodiles were abundant. No one knew for sure what other dangerous wildlife lurked in the waist-deep river water.

I watched Dad paint yellow stripes on trees so he could, he hoped, find his way back through the bush one day. Our nearest neighbor, Bob Gawler, wound his way through the bush to introduce himself. Upon seeing all the yellow paint stripes, he exclaimed, "I thought it was the bloody Stars and Stripes!"

Axes required sharpening every day, and some brush was so hard that our bush-whacking tools were woefully inadequate. Chainsaws were useless owing to the *mopani* ("mo-pawn-nee") hardwoods, which wore away the teeth on the chains in a matter of minutes. The going was agonizing. It took several days to make the last 10 miles.

I will never understand what the hurry was, but my family didn't have time to spend in African language school in the capital of Salisbury, 300 miles away. So, we hired a local interpreter—an old man named Marata, who came highly recommended.

Marata had a standard six-year (eighth grade) education and was literate. His English was minimal, but truth be known, there wasn't an alternative. We rapidly immersed ourselves in the local culture, but the learning curve was steep. The primitive conditions had resulted in a host of bizarre customs. The adaptation was brisk, however, and both the local people and my family embraced each other openly.

At Melelzi, there was no fresh running water. Water was hauled in fifty-five gallon drums from the town of Fort Victoria, 150 miles to

THE BIG MOVE

the north. The drums were held by come-along tie-downs to secure them to the bed of our Dodge Power Wagon. We could not afford to lose one precious drop of clean water. Petrol and diesel were transported the same way.

At the new mission site, bricks were made by first creating mud from dried clay obtained from the abundant ant/termite hills and then pouring the mud mixture into wooden forms and firing them in a cavernous homemade kiln. The bricks were needed to build the first school, which also would serve as the church educational building. The second building would be a medical clinic.

Initially, there was no permanent shelter for us, so our first domicile was a canvas lean-to with mosquito netting over the cots. Within a few months, a thatch hut was built to house our family. The hut had no door. The Africans were curious about these strange newcomers and would drive their cattle within inches of the hut's opening, just to have a look at us. On one such cattle drive, I looked out the door to see a white girl with blonde hair, who was taking a herd to the water. I ran out among all of the long-horns calling for her. "Hey, slow down," I called out. I was so excited. I wanted to know what she was doing clear out there. But she ignored me. I kept calling out to her. When I finally reached her, I could see she was severely sunburned and had deep scabs on her lips and face from sun damage. She still wouldn't talk to me.

Disappointed, I walked back to our hut. Mum explained that the young girl was an albino and that they were looked down upon. Most times, she said, because of health issues, albinos didn't live to be very old. Curious people weren't the only things drawn to our open-air hut—on more than one occasion, my brother and I would wake up in the morning to find a cobra or mamba close to our cots. We knew not to move, but to call out "snake." Dad would grab the .410 shotgun and quickly kill the unwelcome intruder, and fling it out the open door.

As the months wore on, none of the seasoned missionaries who had vociferously begged and cajoled my parents into opening up a mission at this new location ever came to offer their help or expertise as they'd promised. In fact, none came even to pay a social visit. At no time did colleagues from the established medical mission offer assistance or relief or inquire what additional supplies might be needed. The place was famously known as the "closest place to hell on earth." The mission officials who had recruited us were well aware — they had conveniently failed to share that with the naïve missionary family.

As time wore on, our endeavor grew into a normal fully functioning mission. Diagnosing and treating the local inhabitants' medical needs was hampered by our language barriers — we desperately needed the help of an experienced African to accurately translate medical symptoms and history and to explain treatments to the patients. The interpreter we used for day-to-day work was unfamiliar with medical terminology and often translated incorrectly.

When Dad inquired about the possibility of borrowing a nurse from the main Central Africa Mission hospital, he was told there were none available, or they hadn't finished their training, or they had been promised elsewhere. In reality, none of the African nurses wanted to be sent to a place that even the natives considered the end of the world. Dad also asked for assistance in sending established African preachers to help train new preachers in Maranda Tribal Trust Land. This request was also ignored. He sent yet another request asking for assistance in securing Bibles and hymnbooks in the Shona language. Again, this request went unanswered.

Finally, Dad drove to Salisbury, 300 miles away, and found a publisher of Shona Bibles and personally purchased two dozen of them. Next, he contacted the Church of Sweden, which had translated many of the hymns into the natives' Shona language, and, since the costs were well over his supplies budget, he used personal funds to purchase several dozen paperbound hymnals.

Until the medical facility building was completed, clinic hours were held each morning under a large tree adjacent to the eventual site. Sterilization of needles and syringes was accomplished by

THE BIG MOVE

boiling water over an open fire in front of our hut—needles were a scarce resource so when they became dull, they were sharpened with an emery board.

Nighttime emergencies were frequent. Dad sutured head wounds and treated snakebites by the light of a small paraffin lantern held by Mum or my brother and me. (The lantern was the sole source of light we had.) The oily emission from the wick of the lantern would create black soot on the globe, so periodically the lamp would have to be extinguished and the glass globe cleaned. While Dad waited in the darkness for the newly clean globe to appear, he conversed with patients in an effort to learn about their culture.

Many of the women had three round scars on both cheeks, one dot on the top and the other two side by side below, creating a triangle. To create this artwork, the skin was sliced and then packed with a little dirt, creating perfectly round scars at the vertices of the triangle. This same pattern was often also created about their breasts and waists, exemplifying additional masterful artwork, a part of their unique culture.

Often, I would accompany my parents to a village to help with a delivery in distress, e.g. a breech presentation. We would arrive to find the woman sitting on a smooth cow dung-covered floor in a hut, propped up by an *mbuya* (grandmother). The smoke from the fire would be so thick that our eyes would burn and our noses would run. Dozens of flies would settle onto the eyes and noses of everyone in the hut. It was nearly impossible to brush them off.

In this early time, we became all too familiar with African-on-African violence. One morning, Dad was asked to come help a child who had been burned in a fire. I wanted to jump in the truck and go with him, but Dad, sensing this was not something he wanted his baby girl to be exposed to, said no. My brother, two years my senior, accompanied him. Mum stayed behind with me. When they arrived at the village, they found a hut still smoldering, its thatch roof collapsed. The child, about twelve years of age, was reduced to a charred corpse. Dad couldn't even determine the sex of the child.

HOTDOGS for HYENAS

This had been a brutal act of retaliation. The door to the hut had been locked while the child was sleeping and a petrol bomb tossed on the thatch roof. No amount of training or experience could have prepared any of us for the brutality of the African bush.

Before leaving for Africa, my parents had researched what medical supplies would be needed. They estimated in advance that we would need three full years of supplies, because we would not be able to get additional funds and heavy equipment. Among the purchases were dozens of 55-gallon drums, each of which was lined with plastic and tightly packed with medical supplies. Metal rings were added to allow for padlocking. After spray-painting our destination on the outside of the barrels, we shipped them by freighter from Oregon to Cape Town via the Panama Canal.

Once the supplies arrived at the port in South Africa, we were notified by mail. Dad arranged for customs clearance, paying exorbitant fees for the new supplies. From the point of disembarkation in Cape Town, the supplies were then transported to Southern Rhodesia by rail.

In one of our interviews, Dad said, "That was an expensive practical lesson to learn." After that, any supplies being shipped from the States were declared "used" and of negligble monetary value, even if they were in their original packaging.

During these early years of treating patients, Dad began the process of blending African culture and *muti* (medicine) with traditional Western treatment. He astutely recognized that to convert the African natives to Christians, he would first need to earn their trust. This could be accomplished only after he established bonds of friendship and mutual respect. So, instead of taking a Western stance and instantly discounting traditional African healing methods, he listened intently to what tribal elders told him. It bothered my parents greatly that the other mission sites seemed to treat the native Africans as nearly subhuman and made little effort to communicate on their terms or in their language. Seeing this, it was of little surprise to him that the penetration of Christian theology remained inconsequential.

THE BIG MOVE

Dad knew what he wanted to accomplish—he wanted to introduce Christianity by example.

In addition to having a limited water supply, we had no refrigeration. Our meat supply came from hunting game, such as kudu, impala, *duiker* (pronounced die-kah), and *steenbok*. Every member of our family became adept at handling firearms, tracking game, and skinning what we shot. Mum became the official butcher. What wasn't cooked right away was cut into strips and dried into a form of jerky called *biltong*.

Hunting game to feed the family began at an early age. My brother, Mike, at age 13, was already a skilled hunter.

Communication with the outside world was extremely limited. It took nearly three weeks for precious letters from America to reach us. Once a week, we drove 75 miles through the bush to the closest tar road. The driver of a bus, overloaded with passengers carrying everything from firewood to chickens, would stop at this junction, stirring up a blanket of choking dust, would throw out a gray canvas mailbag with a padlock at the top and wait for us to hand him the outgoing mailbag containing letters returning to America.

As soon as my brother and I were able to handle a motorcycle (around the age of ten), we were sent out by ourselves through the bush trails to meet the mail bus to save our parents from losing a full day in the clinic.

HOTDOGS for HYENAS

On one such trip, we ran out of gas 12 miles from home. Michael grabbed the handlebars and pushed while I placed my hands against the back seat and did my part to get through areas with heavy sand. A couple miles into our trek, we noticed great big tracks right in the middle of our path. Neither my brother nor I said anything to each other. Each of us hoped the other hadn't seen the tracks. After all, we had no door to shut, even if we came face to face with the lion that was ahead of us.

At one point, the tracks veered off to the right and our eyes shifted in that direction. I expected at any moment to meet my maker. Then, in a little clearing we saw her—between the lioness's front legs was the carcass of a freshly killed goat. She was looking at us, too, but wasn't interested in us since we offered no threat to her prize. We didn't even whisper to one another the rest of the way home.

On another trip, we spun out in some heavy sand. In order to help balance the bike, I took my feet off the pegs and stuck them straight out. Thwaak, I hit a tree with my foot.

That caused Mike to lose the last semblance of control of the bike. I catapulted off and skidded, face down, on the ground, tearing the skin off my chin. When I tried to walk, I discovered my toe was broken, too.

Since Mike was older and considered to be somewhat responsible for me, I didn't want him to get in trouble for our little prang. I couldn't disguise my chin, but I silently walked on the broken toe for weeks, never telling the parents.

It was generally dark by the time we returned on mail run days. We would gather around lantern light and carefully open the lightweight blue aerogram letters. Other than through broadcasts of the Voice of America on shortwave radio, these letters were our only source of American news.

After a few months, we began building the first school for African children in Melelzi and recruited African teachers from the Central Africa Mission teachers college. Shortly after the school opened, drought plagued the area and starvation set in. The government distributed dried milk, mealie meal, and dried peas in fifty-pound bags to the schools. The distribution, however, was not exactly a door-to-door operation. Dad and I drove 75 miles to receive our ration of dried food and handed it over to the head teacher.

But the physical conditions of the school children continued to deteriorate. Their small bellies were distended to pregnancy size, their faces were gaunt, their legs spindly, and their hair was turning an ochre-reddish color. The children were still attending school, but Dad wondered out loud how they could even focus on their studies.

He began questioning the children and discovered they were not receiving their allotments of the much-needed food. Dad and I immediately rushed to the teacher's hut, where after he kicked in the door, we found nearly all the food shipped over the past two months stacked from floor to ceiling. The teacher was selling the food to local adults for a sizable profit.

Every one of us had a responsibility to help with teaching, regardless of age.

Dad let the interloper know, transcending any cultural divide in language, that after the sacrifices we had made to bring the Word of God to Africa, we were *not* going to be derailed by a selfish, petty thief. He summarily loaded the teacher and his belongings into his truck and drove him the two-day trip back to the Central Africa Mission headquarters. He never hired another teacher from that organization.

It deeply disappointed us that a native African would permit his own students to suffer malnutrition and permanent brain damage in exchange for the paltry income from these stolen rations. Dad was amazed that personal greed could rise to this brutal level. He'd risked his life and the welfare of his entire family for the good of black Africans, yet they could not be fair to one another.

Thus, began the first of many disappointments in the long and steadily eroding relationship between us and the established missionaries under the umbrella of Central Africa Mission. It was not the warm, receptive indigenous locals that frustrated our efforts. It was the infrastructure—the missionaries, politicians, bureaucrats and our fellow Americans who were undermining us. The actual natives were every bit as pure in their hearts as we were.

Eventually, we moved from the open-air hut to a nearby *kopje* (pronounced "copy"), a granite outcropping / small mountain that jutted vertically from the ground to a height of as much as 250 feet. The vistas from the top offered views of the African bush and breathtaking panoramas of the brilliant nighttime sky. We gradually constructed additional structures, including a few outbuildings, a stone patio, an outhouse, a chicken pen, and a trash pit. Mum planted a garden to provide fresh produce for the family on the flat plateau adjacent to the rocky peaks. Our camper became the kitchen and dining area. Owing to the tropical climate, the growing season in southern Africa is virtually all year long.

Snakes and scorpions were in wide abundance on the *kopje*. We learned to shake out our shoes every morning before slipping into them to avoid the venomous sting of the indigenous scorpions.

THE BIG MOVE

All water sources were infected with parasites, so Dad ran a pipeline from a nearby catch dam to the top of the *kopje* rock face, where he placed a metal tank on a trestle he purchased at a store 250 miles away. He installed a diesel water pump to periodically fill the tank and added chlorination. Gravity fed the potable water from the elevated tank to various structures.

The dam was filled by runoff only during the peak of the rainy season in December and January. As the season wore on, the local cattle would wade farther out into the water, excreting bodily wastes into our precious water supply. Eventually the water would dry up, and the ground would crack, exposing huge crevices.

The open-air clinic continued to be the site for administering medical care. Before dawn, patients would climb the rocky *kopje* and quietly wait to be treated for ailments ranging from diarrhea to impetigo, lacerations, python bites, third-degree burns, fractures, malaria, and bilharzia parasites.

Clothing was scarce for the people; diapers were unheard of for children. And with the scarcity of water, it was often difficult to clean up patients who had arrived at the clinic already incredibly ill, covered in feces and vomit.

At this time Dad began to research the common local ailment, an infection with parasitic flatworms called *schistosomiasis*, or as it is known in Africa, *bilharzia*. Every day, he saw the effects of it in the schoolchildren. Their responses in the classroom were unusually slow, and they complained of bloody diarrhea. Dad said, "Knowing that bilharzia was a water-borne parasite, initially I believed I could eradicate it in thirty days. When my initial extermination plan failed, I thought I could solve the health issue regarding bilharzia within six months. By following two simple rules, the people of Maranda Tribal Trust Land could be delivered from this dreadful disease. The first step would be for everyone to quit peeing in the infested water. The second step would be for everyone to quit wading in the water. Why was this so difficult for everyone to understand and implement?"

Bilharzia was named after the nineteenth-century German physician Theodor Bilharz (1825–62). While working in Egypt in 1851, Bilharz discovered the cestode worm *Hymenolepis nana* in the small intestine of a patient. That same year he discovered the trematode worm that is the cause of urinary schistosomiasis.

The life cycle of these parasitic worms is complex. A form of the parasite (the cercaria form) is released from a snail. It burrows into a person's skin, usually when he or she is wading in the water. There is generally an itchiness at the site where the parasite has made entry.

From there it transforms to another stage. It then migrates to another location — the urinary tract, the liver, or the intestine — where the adult worms develop. Eggs are shed by the adult worms into the urinary tract or the intestine which hatch to form miracidia (still another form of the parasite). When the person pees in the water, he or she re-infects the snails, completing the cycle.

Upon learning the scientific basis for this endemic infestation, Dad created a program to wipe out bilharzia by educating the children in the mission schools. While the women carried the majority of the water to the villages from the water hole or river, school-age children were generally with them or were delegated this responsibility at a very early age.

Dad believed that if the children were educated through several academic avenues, they would be the instrument of change, helping implement a healthier outlook and longevity for the people. During science classes, the children studied the two-host multi-stage parasite. They took field trips to the watering site and identified the snail that was the initial host. They were able to create graphs to diagram the journey of schistosomiasis through the body. The schoolchildren were even able to incorporate bilharzia into art class and a school play. They found that they, their families, and their environment were a living, breathing laboratory.

Dad was convinced that once educated, the people could easily eradicate the disease, so the next step was to educate patients at the clinic. While patients were waiting on the veranda and in the yard of

THE BIG MOVE

the clinic, African nurses communicated to them the steps that needed to be taken to eliminate bilharzia. Town hall-type conversations developed on the steps of the clinic.

The community seemed to understand what their responsibilities would be. It would take a partnership to wipe out the disease. Prevention—boiling drinking and bathing water (which would require they no longer use the backwater to bathe in) was discussed repeatedly. Again, field trips to the water hole were arranged to take patients through the process visually.

Hoping to see a drop in cases, we tracked numbers month after month. Sadly, however, there was never a reduction in the amount of medicine needed to treat patients diagnosed with the disease.

Another issue that deeply troubled my parents was the marginalization of African women. Any form of venereal disease was referred to as "women's disease."

Dad set about to change that misconception. Men would come to the clinic to ask for treatment—never women—so the clinic refused to administer treatment until a man brought all his wives and sexual partners to the clinic. They all had to be treated at the same time.

This great equalizer set the precedent that treatment was a family issue, which began with the family unit. The main responsibility rested firmly on the husband. After this protocol was established, treatment became a social event. Laughter could often be heard from the participants as they lined up to receive their penicillin shots.

Even so, the treatment of women as chattel continued to concern my family. If a woman was believed to have been unfaithful, retribution was swift and violent. One particular case reached the depth of my soul.

One morning, I was standing next to Dad when we met a patient in her teens struggling to walk up the steps of the clinic. She was leaning on the arm of an old man.

Normally, African women have a high threshold for pain, but this woman's pain was so intolerable, tears were streaming down her face and she screamed in agony. Blood ran down the insides of the young woman's legs. What really captured my attention were the burn holes in her tattered, blood-drenched skirt.

The young woman continued to cry out as she shuffled barefoot into the clinic. She lay down on the floor—sitting was impossible.

Dad spoke to the old man. "Do you know her?"

"She lives in my *kraal*."

"Do you know what happened?"

"The women said she was cooking and suddenly fell close to the fire."

"Has she ever done this before?" Dad wanted to eliminate the possibility of seizure.

"Perhaps. Otherwise, I don't know."

"Is this your daughter?"

"No."

"Why did you bring her?"

"This is my youngest wife. You must make her better."

Two assistants lay the teen on the examining table. I was hit by a wave of nausea as dad found the source of the bleeding. Her legs were clean of trauma. What had once been her vaginal area was an unrecognizable bloody pulp of tissue.

"Who did this to her?"

"She was very bad."

The old man finally divulged that his young wife had been unfaithful. No doubt he'd had help in having the young woman's legs spread apart while he took a burning *mopani* pole and forced it into her vagina. Dad was sickened but knew he had to use this as a valuable teaching moment. He made it clear that the young woman would not be able to have children. The *lobola* (bride-price) the old man had paid for the young woman had been wasted. In this chattel-based system, the old man had only himself to blame. He had not cared for his investment.

4
MISSION SITE NUMBER 1

Opening up new missions involved an exorbitant amount of bureaucratic red tape. And although my family had been told by the existing missionaries that the permits had been properly applied for and approved, precious little had been accomplished.

The local district commissioner (DC) at Nuanetsi, Alan Wright, was pushing for more schools to be opened in Maranda Tribal Trust Land. Initially, the professional relationship between DC Wright and Dad was cordial. However, before we arrived in Southern Rhodesia, Wright had several verbal "knockdown" fights with another missionary from Central Africa Mission, John Pemberton.

This should have been a red flag for us—for what was in store for my entire family. Wright was greatly angered over the arrogance of Pemberton, who had attempted to bully his way into establishing rights to a mission site in Maranda Tribal Trust Land. We were unaware of the tenuous situation preceding our arrival, and Wright did not understand that we and Pemberton were both under the same mission umbrella, Central Africa Mission, when approving Dad's mission application.

During one meeting between Dad and Wright, my brother Mike was waiting outside the commissioner's Nuanetsi outpost. After seeing Pemberton unexpectedly pull up to the office, Mike innocently sauntered into where the meeting was taking place and announced, "Pemberton is here." All hell broke loose. Wright immediately assumed the two were there to dish out perceived American entitlement. He became angry and demanded Pemberton leave his office.

The relationship between DC Wright and Dad deteriorated from that point. Wright would send a messenger on bicycle nearly 70 miles one way to summon Dad to his office at his Nuanetsi headquarters. Upon arriving, Dad would sit on the veranda for an extended period, waiting for an audience with Wright, only to be admonished that he had not filled out some obscure governmental paperwork correctly or to find that Wright had gone to tea and was unavailable.

In response to Wright's push to have more schools built, Dad argued it was fruitless to establish schools when a permanent site had not been granted. Wright, a devout Catholic with *Pommie* (Englishman) inclinations, expressed his disdain for itinerant Yankees at every opportunity. He had been unsuccessful in his personal efforts to have a Catholic presence in Maranda Tribal Trust Land. Now he had to deal with not only a Yankee but a *Protestant* Yankee.

During the conferences with Wright, Dad realized the commissioner was truly uninterested in serving the African population he was being paid to represent. "It was evident that Wright was lying sideways in the public trough," he said. "After each meeting Wright would say, 'Are you still wasting your time trying to save those *kaffirs* (unbelievers) over on Maranda?'"

The issue of safe drinking water for the family, clinic, and schools reached a critical point. Dad hired a geologist to identify the best site for a borehole (well). It became clear that this endeavor would be cost-prohibitive. A depth of 850 feet would have to be reached, and there was still no guarantee that the water source, even if tapped, would be reliable. And, the costs to drill to that depth were a formidable financial barrier. So, we continued to pump filthy backwater from the dam for the needs of the mission. To make the water safe to drink, we pumped it into to an overhead tank and used alum to settle the debris, followed by heavy chlorination.

5
LOSING MISSION NUMBER 1

After two years of our putting down roots, the government, in its usual arbitrary and unpredictable fashion, would not grant our fervently prayed for permanent mission site. In addition, they offered no compensation for our two years at hard labor, building substantial infrastructure at the site.

The initial negotiations between my parents and the government had begun with Dad traveling the 300 miles to the capital of Salisbury. It was not unusual for delays of six months to be imposed without explanation. Despite the fact this fledgling mission was under the umbrella of the Central Africa Mission, however, Dad hammered out an initial agreement with the government alone.

During one of his negotiation trips to Salisbury, Dad and I were returning to the mission at night. The air was clear and cold (by Zimbabwean standards), and the sky was brilliant with billions of stars. We were 100 miles from civilization when suddenly, our truck skidded across the road and came to a rest in a ditch. The bolts on the wheels of the truck had sheared off.

Strip roads, where a narrow strip of pavement is laid out for each pair of wheels, were the norm for all roads between towns. The center between the strips was dirt and when two oncoming cars met, if a driver did not slow down before crossing over to a single strip, he could easily run off the road.

HOTDOGS FOR HYENAS

Strip roads

We decided we would have to spend the night in the cab of the truck and walk for help in the morning. We could not sleep on the exposed flat-bed on the back of the truck because of known packs of roving carnivorous hyenas.

During the night, unexpected help came in the form of a government transportation employee who happened upon our disabled vehicle. Dad asked that the man take me to safety—he would stay with the truck.

The employee, who lived in a remote outpost, loaded me and my black-and-tan Doberman puppy into his Land Rover and drove us to his house. I felt sad about my father being left alone by the road. My obvious distress tore at the heartstrings of this Good Samaritan, and he drove the 20 miles back and collected Dad. We had a hot meal, a shower, and clean sheets, and the next morning got the truck back into running shape and finished the trek back to our mission.

After many months of negotiations had stalled, Wright sent a messenger on bicycle 70 miles to ask my father to come immediately

LOSING MISSION NUMBER 1

for an emergency meeting. Dad dropped everything and made the two-hour journey to the Nuanetsi outpost.

Upon his arrival, Wright delivered the government notice that the Melelzi site had been turned down in its quest for a permanent mission. We had only 30 days to negotiate for a new site or leave Africa entirely. Dad's long, lonely trip home to break this devastating news to us was heart-wrenching. We had left American civilization and learned how to fend for ourselves in primitive southern Africa, and now the meager but warm and homey environment we had carved out for ourselvs was pulled out from under us.

After the loss of the mission site at Melelzi, no one from Central Africa Mission was willing to help us emotionally, physically, or spiritually. No one came to check up on us, volunteer to help us move, or even wrote letters of encouragement.

My parents had stepped out on a platform of faith, believing that the call to serve in Africa would be fruitful. Every night before they had prayer and went to bed, Dad and Mum would sigh and say to each other, "We survived another day." Literal survival had become the major achievement of each day.

Dad began to question whether having placed his family in extraordinary and austere living conditions had been worth it. "I thought I was going to save the world," he would tell me later. "I had a plan. I was wrong."

Back in America, our supporters could not fathom our nearly impossible living conditions. The living-link supporting churches anxiously looked forward to receiving monthly letters updating them of the progress. Most of our letters arrived nearly a month after they were sent—by that time, challenges and emergency situations had usually been resolved. All the congregations could do was offer prayers that whatever happened on the mission field would be God's will.

We knew that the work we had begun at Melelzi would unravel once we moved. Despite our many challenges, the mission provided numerous valuable services to the surrounding community. The school, constructed from handmade bricks, had several classrooms; more than one grade could be taught in each room. As the schoolchildren gathered outside for morning exercise and sports, patients gathered in one of the classrooms for triage. The floors were scrubbed daily with the strong disinfectant of Dettol (a powerful brand of disinfectant used even to wash down vehicles passing through hoof-and-mouth-disease endemic areas) before the children came in for morning lessons.

The classrooms were opened again for clinic hours after the children were dismissed in the afternoon. It was common for people to walk 20 miles or be driven by donkey cart to be seen by us. When Dad received a message that someone was too ill to be brought to the clinic, he drove great distances to reach them.

Once a week, preaching classes were held at the school for the aspiring future African preachers. From the mission's primitive and inauspicious beginnings, there were now eight churches established within Maranda Tribal Trust Land. The African preachers, armed with Shona Bibles and sermons, dispersed to different locations to preach the Word. Some of the services were held in a village, but the majority were held under shade trees within close proximity of several villages.

The school at Melelzi was used on Sunday for church services, Sunday school, and sewing classes, and became a hub of diverse community activities.

The Shona tribe of Maranda Tribal Trust Land was known to be a peaceful people. Originally an offshoot of the Venda tribe of the Transvaal (South Africa), they had lived in the same vicinity of the Lowveld for nearly a hundred years. They'd initially found the land they now occupied vacant and had simply settled and taken possession of it. They fought no battle over it and apparently were never raided by the neighboring Ndebele or Shangaan tribes.

Maranda Tribal Trust Land encompassed nearly 250,000 acres of intricately-balanced rock outcroppings — *kopjes* — and endless stands of *mopani* trees. For years, it had been considered land owned by the

LOSING MISSION NUMBER 1

British Crown and occupied by African squatters.

Shortly before our arrival, in the late-1950s, the government decided to regulate the land, making it into an official African tribal area. Immediately after our arrival, Dad had begun making inroads with local headmen and the chief, who was appropriately named Chief Maranda. He often visited tribal villages and could be seen sitting on the ground sharing a meal of *sadza* (white mealie meal placed in boiling water and cooked to a thick porridge), discussing the needs of the people and he often took me with him. I was fairly fluent in more than one of the African languages and would wander around the village talking to the mothers and eating great chunks of watermelon that had been dropped on their cow-dung kitchen floors.(This was the norm for cutting up melon and often took some skill to maneuver through the seeds and flies. They all looked the same to me.)

At the end of these visits, it was usual for me to be given a gift of a chicken (and to generally arrive home covered in lice *from* the chicken). The gift of the chicken signified the tremendous respect the people had for our missionary family. In this extremely poor agrarian culture, one chicken could feed an entire village. Instead it was given to us as an expression of gratitude.

With the forced and unexpected closing of the first mission site, Dad was summoned to Chief Maranda's *kraal*. The old chief was short in stature (five foot three, at best) but had tremendous authority over the tribe. He handled his own tribal court cases, normally making a judgment without contacting the Nuanetsi police — 50 miles away — to make an arrest. If a person was caught stealing a cow, for example, the victim received *two* cows from the thief, and the chief was given a cow as well. If a man was accused of adultery, the chief would sleep with the man's wife (or his multiple wives, in the case of a polygamist).

On one occasion, Chief Maranda was riding in the Dodge truck with Dad. Many of the villages were built extremely close to the road, and on this occasion, a *bundu* dog ran out in front of the truck.

HOTDOGS FOR HYENAS

Bundu dogs hung around the villages. They were the size and shape of greyhounds and were typically severely malnourished. They were hardly valued as family pets. If they came close to the fire or the food, they were guaranteed to have a rock thrown at them.

Dad stopped the moment the dog ran in front of the truck, but it was too late—the dog had been killed immediately. Dad got out of the truck, and the *baba* (father) of the village began exclaiming that the dead dog was his most valuable possession, demanding restitution.

At that point, Chief Maranda exited the truck and stepped in front of the man, who immediately recognized him. The old chief knelt down and flipped the dead dog's ear back. Dogs who received rabies shots were given a tattoo in the ear, identifying the year the shot was received. This dog had no tattoo.

Chief Maranda raised his head and looked at the man. "Did your dog receive a rabies shot last Monday at the cattle dip tank?"

The village baba shook his head. "No."

"Did you not have a collar and lead on your dog?"

"No."

The conversation was quickly heading in a ridiculously funny direction, considering that it was being held in the middle of the bush.

"There is a fencing-in law here in this country," said the chief. "It means that all livestock must be fenced in so they will not get into someone else's property, maize field, village, or road. Does this dog belong to you?"

The baba lowered his head. "Yes."

The chief considered the man and then pronounced his judgment. "Then I should fine you, because your livestock ran out into the road, hitting the truck, and could have injured us. But today, I am feeling very generous. I will let you off with a warning."

And with that Chief Maranda and Dad resumed their trip.

Our time at the mission was coming to a close and we were concerned about who would sustain it after we were gone. Then Chief Maranda sent word that he wanted to see Dad. As he arrived at Chief Maranda's *kraal*, he saw the old chief shuffling toward the truck to

LOSING MISSION NUMBER 1

meet him. They gave each other the traditional African handshake by shaking once, clasping each other's thumb, and then shaking again. Before they got to the chief's agenda, however, the following ritual was followed:

> *Chief Maranda:* "*Mangwanani, Umfundisi.*" ("Good morning, Teacher.")
> *Dad:* "*Mangwanani, Chief Maranda.*" ("Good morning.")
> *Chief Maranda:* "*Makadeni?*" ("How are you?")
> *Dad:* "*Tinofara. Makadeni?*" ("I am well. How are you?")
> *Chief Maranda:* "*Tinofara. Mamuka sei?*" ("I am well. Did you get up?")
> *Dad:* "*Tamuka. Mamuka sei?*" ("I did. Did you get up?")
> *Chief Maranda:* "*Tamuka wo.*" ("I got up as well.")

Once the prelude to conversation was concluded, Chief Maranda, who generally enjoyed an early-morning brew of slimy homemade *doro* (beer), began the dialogue.

"You are our Moses," he said. "You have been sent to us. I have visited the schools, and the children are learning. I have seen the people being healed by your muti. The children in the Sunday school are singing many songs; the people are better because they know about your God. I want to help you. I will make sure the children will still go to school and pay any fees. I will send the people to you, wherever you are, for the muti. If you come back once a week, I will make sure all of the sick people are here on that day. *Asi* [But] I would like to have a church service to now be held at my village. I want the people of Maranda to know that my village is a place where people can learn about Jesus. I want them to know that someone died for them, and he is coming back to take them to heaven."

Dad said nothing and the chief continued. "I will send the preachers to you by bicycle so they can learn from you and they can return to us to preach."

HOTDOGS FOR HYENAS

Through years of patient waiting, Dad had miraculously achieved the trust and confidence of the leader of the Maranda Tribal Trust. When he returned home that evening, a student was waiting for him.

Fihla Mtimkulu had been raised in a village not far from the mission. His father had four wives; Fihla's mother was his first wife. Tall, thin, and well spoken, he told Dad how much he had benefited from the mission school and said he had decided to attend the teachers college in Bulawayo. He would return, he said, on all school holidays to substitute-teach at the mission school and to help spread the Gospel on Sunday, baptizing the new followers and, after he finished his three-year training at the teachers college, he would return to Maranda Tribal Trust Land and be the head teacher for his people.

He was as good as his word. Fihla Mtimkulu did return to teach and later became the headmaster of the schools, where he worked for forty years before retiring. Because of Headmaster Mtimkulu's ability to become an educational role model for the people of Maranda, he influenced countless others—young students and parents recognized the supreme value of education, the status it brought to the community, and the associated financial benefits to the family and the region. Eventually, more students followed the progressive path now available to them. Many used the local education as a springboard, continuing on to teachers colleges and nursing schools and gaining university degrees. A few obtained degrees in medicine and continue to practice in Zimbabwe and South Africa.

Another student, Roda, was sent to nursing school run by The Church of Sweden's mission hospital. She had benefited greatly from her mission-school education. She too wanted to serve the people of Maranda and my parents paid for her nursing school education.

The day she completed her training, she returned by bus to the bush. Fresh in her nurse's uniform and cap, she went to work ministering medically to her own people. A year later, she married Fihla Mtimkulu and worked for 40 years beside him.

As news reached the people—via bush telegraph—that the government had declined to allow the establishment of a permanent

LOSING MISSION NUMBER 1

mission, the people of Melelzi ignored the directive and continued to make their way to see us on a daily basis. They offered not just their support but also whatever they could do to ensure the church, the school, and the clinic—all essential components of a mission—continued.

Regina Dube, a deaconess in the church, said she would continue to prepare communion every Sunday and would teach Bible classes for the women. Regina had attended school at the Lundi Mission (Free Methodist) over 100 miles away, graduating with a standard six-year (eighth grade) education. Her husband, a schoolteacher, continued to teach at Lundi, and came home several times a year. Regina maintained the small village they called home, raising crops and taking care of their three children. She had incredible leadership qualities, and the people in the community looked to her for guidance. She filled the leadership vacuum and evolved into a role model for generations to come.

6
MISSION SITE NUMBER 2

Following the Rhodesian government's denial of the initial mission site, a second site was finally agreed upon. Site 2 was close to the Nuanetsi River, 35 miles away from the first site — and required a two-and-half-hour drive through the dense bush.

District Commissioner Wright had enthusiastically encouraged us to move to this site, stating he would locally approve this decision with full recommendation for the government to authorize the new mission. I went with Dad as he hand-carried DC Wright's recommendation to the capital city of Salisbury, 300 miles away. We walked to the Meikles Hotel for tea, sweets and celebration.

After several days, the documents were signed — it was official. The new mission would include 100 acres. All present and future mission houses, clinics, shops, and generator sheds would be constructed close to the river. Filled with anticipation and hope, we moved to the new site. Once again, we were living in the elements. We still had the camper, but with temperatures often over 100 degrees, the interior of the camper became excruciatingly hot.

My brother Mike and I, both always good natured, built beds out of wooden doors, rolled out sleeping bags, and slept soundly. Often, we would wake up in the morning to find hungry white ants (termites) tunneling across the old wood and within hours, the doors (and our beds) would be decimated.

HOTDOGS FOR HYENAS

Dad had purchased a Cessna 180 from Alaska and had it shipped from New Orleans, Louisiana, to Cape Town, South Africa. An airstrip was planned a mile from the river on a flat plateau.

Dad immediately hired a crew to cut down over 3,800 trees and burn stumps and roots to make way for a runway. He knew he could land and take off in 850 feet (uncomfortably), but he needed 2,000 feet for safety and to allow other medical personnel to get in and out safely. With overruns, he was able to reach the desired (and government-mandated) safe-landing and takeoff distances. One end of the runway had a 450-foot granite *kopje*. The river was at the other end.

Upon completion of the airfield, the Department of Aviation flew in to inspect it. After a few changes, the airfield was operational, but it had not yet been completely fenced in. One of the first crises with the new airfield occurred when shepherd boys drove their cattle out on the middle of the runway.

The airfield

It was a great sport for them to see Dad buzz the cattle off the runway. He would fly in low enough to scatter the herd, bank, and come back around the pattern, ready to land. By then, the shepherd boys would drive the cattle back onto the airstrip. On one occasion, when he was getting low on fuel, following a trip from South Africa, he managed to land between two herds. The fencing was completed immediately after that incident.

Even then, however, we would often find sagging gaps in the fencing and droppers, which were often pilfered by local villagers to make cooking pot stands. The villagers would laugh when we'd

MISSION SITE NUMBER 2

come to collect the steel posts, and because it was technically not stealing, no hard feelings were expressed on either side.

Patients could now be airlifted to hospitals in the city and, after the runway was extended, doctors from the Central Africa Mission could fly in to assist. But no one from the organization ever came.

We began massive building projects — trucking in bags of cement from the city of Bulawayo, 250 miles away. Dad hired a crew to make concrete blocks for building us a smaller home that would be used later as a guesthouse. Every morning, he would drive the crew to the dry riverbed. They would shovel sand, filling up the bed of the truck to later mix with the cement.

While in his 40s, Dad shoveled alongside the crew. Shovel full by shovel full, he stayed in rhythm with the much younger workers. For our safety, it was important that the community knew that Dad was strong. It became almost a competition and he commented a time or two that he was nearly shoveled under the truck. But his strength equated to respect.

Being able to break tool handles was considered to be a show of strength for the workers. However, they never said *they* had broken the handle. The answer to how it happened was a normal cultural response: "It broke." But, after a while, "It broke" became expensive. A broken shovel, axe or sledgehammer was out of commission until it could be replaced.

Finally, to stop the breakage, Dad began welding shorter steel-rod handles. With that problem solved, he was able to build a shop, a grease pit, a storeroom, and a generator shed that was 12 feet long.

Dad hired a man named Coinius to build the generator shed. Coinius came with his own tools, including a level. Coinius's level turned out to be "somewhat bent," and when completed, the building was a foot out of square. Together, they adjusted the problem. Dad reasoned that if you live in a round hut, it is sometimes difficult to understand the importance of an in-square shed.

This was another learning moment.

Next, we began building a second school. This primary school was close to the airfield. We were able to pump water to it through a four-inch galvanized pipe from a water hole in the Nuanetsi River. Once again, the water was infested with bilharzia. Workers had to take great care when connecting the pumps so as not to get water on the skin. In addition, a 12-foot crocodile occupied the water hole. Occasionally, the croc would drag a goat under the water. Sadly, on one occasion, a child playing too close to the edge also became fodder for the massive reptile.

It was during this time that Rhodesia voted for the Unilateral Declaration of Independence (UDI, November 1965) from Great Britain. The country, previously named for John Cecil Rhodes and known for its vast mineral wealth, had prospered since the end of the 19th century. The Federation of Rhodesia (Northern and Southern Rhodesia) and Nyasaland had existed since 1923.

In 1964, Northern Rhodesia was granted independence from Great Britain, becoming the nation of Zambia, and power was transferred to black rule. Nyasaland, now Malawi, did the same. Southern Rhodesia considered a transfer of power to the black majority to be an economic, political, and tribal disaster for all Rhodesian citizens. Then-Prime Minister Ian Smith and the Rhodesian government attempted to negotiate with Great Britain for months on a reasonable compromise, but no solution was reached. But expectations of independence had continued to brew, and finally that day had come.

Dad had taken the truck to Bulawayo for supplies, not knowing that independence was imminent. Back at the mission, Mum, Michael and I gathered around the shortwave radio to hear history being made as Prime Minister Smith addressed the tiny country in a live broadcast. Smith began with this proclamation:

> *Whereas in the course of human affairs history has shown that it may become necessary for a people to resolve the political affiliations which have connected them with another people and to assume among other nations the separate and equal status to which they are entitled:*

MISSION SITE NUMBER 2

And whereas in such event a respect for the opinions of mankind requires them to declare to other nations the causes which impel them to assume full responsibility for their own affairs:

Now therefore, we, the Government of Rhodesia, do hereby declare:

That it is an indisputable and accepted historic fact that since 1923 the Government of Rhodesia have exercised the powers of self-government and have been responsible for the progress, development, and welfare of their people...

Now therefore we, the Government of Rhodesia, in humble submission to Almighty God, who controls the destiny of nations, conscious that the people of Rhodesia have always shown unswerving loyalty and devotion to Her Majesty the Queen and earnestly praying that we the people of Rhodesia will not be hindered in our determination to continue exercising our undoubted right to demonstrate the same loyalty and devotion in seeking to promote the common good so that the dignity and freedom of all men may be assured, do by this proclamation adopt, enact, and give to the people of Rhodesia the Constitution annexed hereto. God Save the Queen...

I call upon all of you in this historic hour to support me and my government in the struggle in which we are engaged. I believe that we are a courageous people and history has cast us in a heroic role. To us has been given the privilege of being the first Western nation in the last two decades to have the determination and fortitude to say: "So far and no further." We may be a small country, but we are a determined people who have been called upon to play a role of worldwide significance. We Rhodesians have rejected the doctrinaire philosophy of appeasement and surrender. The decision which we have taken today is a refusal by Rhodesians to sell their birthright. And, even if we were to surrender, does anyone believe that Rhodesia would be the last target of the communists in the Afro-Asian bloc?

We have struck a blow for the preservation of justice, civilization, and Christianity—and in the spirit of this belief we have thus assumed our sovereign independence.

God bless you all. (Smith, 1997)

HOTDOGS FOR HYENAS

Following the radiocast, with my brother and me gathered around, Mum spoke to our houseboy, Jimius, and explained what had happened. The government had advised that families in isolated areas evacuate to more populated areas until the swirl of political uncertainty subsided.

Peter Scales, a well-known businessman from Bulawayo, flew down to the new mission field to evacuate Mum, Michael and me. The weather had settled in around the mission until there was zero visibility. A light *guti* (misty rain) was falling. We could hear the aircraft circling overhead, but the experienced pilot couldn't find the runway. Unable to reach us, Peter turned around and returned to town, praying that we understood he had attempted to fly us to a safe location. For precautionary purposes, Mum insisted we sleep in the same room that night, with weapons loaded and our dogs close by. The next day, Dad arrived back at the mission.

In retaliation for Rhodesia's declaration of independence, the United Nations declared sanctions on the tiny country. Petrol and sugar rationing were implemented. To secure the existing supply of petrol, the mission's fuel tanks were padlocked at all times.

Supplies chains were cut, including the importation of oil. Rhodesia had previously imported canned goods from other countries, including the United States. These products were no longer available. The store shelves were bare. The people of Rhodesia were hopeful that America would be compassionate toward Rhodesia, considering that the United States itself had declared independence from Great Britain. But the United States agreed with the implementation of sanctions.

Rhodesia began in earnest to become self-sufficient overnight. There was a can-do spirit everywhere. Almost immediately, vegetables and fruits were raised, canned, and labeled within the country. The sugarcane fields began to produce massive quantities of all types of sugar. Molasses was sold to cattle farmers. Nothing was wasted. Even by-products of the cane fields were used to pave roads.

The Rhodesian sense of humor could be seen throughout the country. When toilet paper was produced with the image of Britain's

MISSION SITE NUMBER 2

Prime Minister Harold Wilson stamped on each piece, everyone clamored for a roll, just to have on the coffee table for conversation.

Previously, the movie theaters in town had always played "God Save the Queen" with Queen Elizabeth's picture on the screen before every movie. Everyone would stand and sing in unison. But now, the queen's photo would come up and the music would start. No one stood, No one sang. We all felt we were being extremely daring.

Of course, we kids had our own rendition of the song. "God save our gracious Queen, crown her with paraffin..." I remember my brother propping his feet up on the seat in front of him during this anthem. Occasionally, a couple would still stand and the audience would boo them. This was our only outlet to "show" Britain what we thought.

With Rhodesia standing alone, there was increased concern about terrorist activity. The training of terrorists was taking place in Russia and China, as well as to the north and east of us. Several Africans came to us and said that a man named Mao Zedong promised that if they would fight against the Europeans, he would give them all the lush farmlands. The new recruits were even given small medals to wear with Mao's likeness in the center.

When Dad probed them for more information, though, he learned they had no idea who Mao was. I was around 12 and understood the gravity of the situation and wrote a letter to President Lyndon Johnson in the United States, predicting a tumultuous outcome for Rhodesia.

December 17, 1965

Dear President Johnson,

My name is Pam Courtney, and I am 12 years old. I'm embarrassed to let anyone in my country know that I was born in America. I am writing to let you know what sanctions you and the United Nations have imposed on Rhodesia have done.

Shortly after we declared independence on November 11th, you pulled the American Ambassador out of the capitol of Salisbury and shut down diplomatic relationships. There are many Americans living here — what did that prove? Where are we supposed to go to get travel visas? I expected that you would understand what our tiny country is going through since America did exactly the same thing, declared independence from Great Britain nearly two hundred years ago. You are insisting on majority rule here. Did you abide by that in 1776? Perhaps you should read your own history.

You are bowing to Zambia? Why? Great Britain gave them independence in January. I was there with my brother and friends in the capital of Lusaka. We were forced off of sidewalks and made to walk in the dirt. That's majority rule.

Today, we have petrol rationing and sugar rationing. We are issued stamps for petrol and receive extra rations of petrol and diesel because we live 250 miles from town. We used to be able to get treats such as Libby's fruit cocktail when we went to town once a month. The shelves are bare of canned goods. We are thankful for South Africa and Mozambique for keeping the petrol lines open and transport of goods coming through. When my family needs airplane parts or supplies to treat medical diseases of the local Africans – that won't be possible because of your sanctions.

What you don't understand is that your push for majority rule will throw Rhodesia into chaos. There will be a tribal war between the factions, and no one will survive. We have the Shona and the Sendebele, they do not live peaceably beside each other. Just look at what has happened in other African countries — until the majority of the people understand economics and what makes countries successful, Rhodesia will become the most corrupt nation. It will follow in the footsteps of so many other nations. And what else are you and Great Britain doing by putting pressure on for majority rule? Throwing us into the arms of the Chinese communists. They are already supplying our terrorists with training and giving them medals of Mao Ste Tung. No one knows who Mao is.

I would invite you to come to our country and see for yourself. I'm asking you to reconsider your decision. You are hurting all of

MISSION SITE NUMBER 2

us and it will damage us forever. But I bet you won't. You'd rather pull the ears on your beagles.
   Sincerely yours
   Pam Courtney

Pulling the ears of his beagles was the image of President Johnson presented to us in Africa.

We lived in a country of censorship and my parents always read the letters my brother and I sent out that might be published or picked up by a U.S. newspaper. After reading my letter to President Johnson, Dad said, "Pam, I can't let you send this."

"Why?" I asked.

"Well, our support comes from America. I can't risk losing funding for the mission if someone in the U.S. government doesn't like what you've said."

"But it's all true," I protested. "It's wrong what's happening to us here."

"I'm sorry, Peeky-Deek," said Dad, "but I can't let you mail this."

Being told that I couldn't do something like write a letter about a topic I strongly believed in had a lasting impact on me. The letter was insignificant in the scope of world affairs, and many more interesting things were going on in my young life, but that letter has stuck with me. Years later Dad confessed that he wished he had let me send it.

"You stood on principle," he said.

During this time, the former Prime Minister of Rhodesia, Sir Garfield Todd, was placed under arrest and confined to his ranch for one year. Todd, who had immigrated from New Zealand in the 1930s as a Church of Christ missionary, had paved the way for missionaries under the Central Africa Mission umbrella (which included my parents) to join him in Southern Rhodesia/Rhodesia.

Convoys protecting all of us were common during the Bush War.

My brother and I were friends with Todd's daughter Cynthia. Todd had introduced reforms to give elementary education to every Black African of school age and gave grants to missionary-run schools to introduce secondary schools. He also pushed a bill through the Legislation Assembly allowing for multiracial trade unions.

He was ousted from power for his "over-progressiveness" and when he applied for an exit visa to teach at the University of Edinburgh, the Rhodesian government banned his travel and placed him under house arrest.

MISSION SITE NUMBER 2

This was scary for us kids — we wanted to visit Cynthia. The one time we were allowed to go to the farm, the curtains were drawn in the house and my parents told us not to mention we had been there.

Years later, after Todd donated 3,000 acres of his ranch to former guerrillas who had been maimed in the Rhodesian bush war, President Robert Mugabe stripped Todd of his Zimbabwean nationality.

It was African politics at its finest.

During this time of uneasiness, Dad was proactive — he insisted that Mum maintain target practice with a pistol and rifle to ensure she was respected by everyone. Dad never wanted her to be unprotected when she was alone in the bush. The Africans would say, "Madame can point" — meaning she knew how to handle a gun.

Dad took a "Don't Tread on Me"' stance in order to send a clear message to any terrorist group that the members of our family were capable of protecting ourselves and weren't afraid to shoot.

Other medical missionaries did not share that attitude. One medical doctor in the area said he simply could not bring harm to another human being. Consequently, he and his family, easy targets for terrorist organizations, sought protection and refuge with the police at Nuanetsi, fifty miles away. And the Mao medals? I was riding my horse through a maize field shortly after a rebel fire fight. As I trotted along, I looked down to see a corpse with a Mao medal safety-pinned to his khakis.

"Bugger this," I said to my horse, kicking her in the flank to get away as quickly as we could fly.

Every time I think of that vision, a chill goes up my spine, because today, China controls the economy of this once bountiful and self-sustaining country.

Concerns swirling around the declaration of independence were compounded by the rainy season. As is typical in many Rhodesian rivers, pools of water filled the dry, sandy riverbeds. Often the rains would continue for several days, forcing us to move the pumps to higher ground. During this particular rainy season, the luxury of time eluded us. The Nuanetsi River came down in a wall of water during the night, tearing the Lister diesel pump that supplied the mission's water supply from the concrete pad and dumping it into the bottom of the river.

It would be days before the water subsided. Thankfully, we had water stored in a 250-gallon overhead tank. When the flood waters receded, we dragged the pump out with a winch. The connecting pipes, however, were gone, and we began the task of replacing them. Our lack of access to critical supplies highlighted our vulnerability.

The rainy season also increased the incidence of malaria, which was already rampant in the area. We had often witnessed the devastating effects of cerebral malaria in the people we had come to serve. Seeing children die from malaria was particularly difficult.

Mum was relentless with us, making sure that every Sunday night, we took two chloroquine and one daraprim tablet. This was the worst event of the week to look forward to—there was no disguising the bitter taste of the chloroquine.

Despite this preventive ritual, I became sick with my first bout of malaria. (I had previously been bed-ridden for two months with rheumatic fever.) My parents were stunned—they had been so vigilant about our prevention routine. Not long after recovering from malaria, I had another brush with a near fatal malady. I was confronted with rabies head on.

I had a penchant for dachshunds. The black and tan females that were my constant companions were distinguishable only by the red and green leather collars they wore. Weiner and Schnitzel ran the house and the garden. The slightest uninvited guest would find this tag team tearing out the door to exact justice within their queendom.

One afternoon a *bundu* dog slipped through the gate, down the drive, and around the corner of our generator shed. I yelled for my brother for help as this starving grey-mottled dog loped towards the dachshunds and me with teeth bared. The *bundu* dog latched onto Weiner's neck.

Mike emerged from the house and seeing the chaos, kicked the teeth out of the ferocious *bundu* dog's mouth. Mike got a gun and

MISSION SITE NUMBER 2

shot the *bundu* dog, and taking extreme care, burned the body instead of burying it.

Before I could grab the pups, Schnitzel began licking the wounds from Weiner's floppy ear, but no worry—both dogs were up to date with their rabies vaccinations. Or so we thought. A few evenings later, Schnitzel came into the house frothing at the mouth.

We assumed she had been playing with a frog. The foaming mouth was a normal reaction to "play dates" with frogs. Generally, when this would happen, we would rinse their mouths out and send them on their way.

But this time the dachshund slinked behind the bookcase and the bed. Dad scooped her up and, for the night, put her in a box with a heavy steel grate so we could watch her. In the morning, he said she had not drunk any water and needed to be kept hydrated.

She was docile and compliant, still my sweet dog. I filled my German-made blue metal squirt gun with water and eased the nozzle through the grate. The first day she drank a little bit.

Maybe she just wasn't feeling well, I thought. I continued the routine on a second day, but as I slipped the squirt gun into her mouth, she bit the end of the steel tip clean off. I was in for the long haul, still not comprehending that the dog who had merely licked the saliva off her bitten sister could have contracted rabies. We moved her to a more secure location and I donned welding gloves when I touched her. Then, as I lifted her from her temporary box, she bit straight through to the flesh on my hand and drew blood. We moved her to the generator shed and opened the double doors to allow for fresh air. I took my schoolbooks and sat by her box to keep her hydrated.

Her eyes finally glazed to a greenish tint and she reeked of a sickly-sweet smell. She attacked everything, including me, that came near her box. Ultimately, of course, she died. Upon her death, we immediately took her body to the police station and they rushed it to Salisbury. Examination of her brain revealed she was positive for rabies.

That meant I was likely infected as well. We immediately left for Bulawayo for treatment, which meant 14 shots in the stomach.

The initial shots were administered by nursing students at the hospital. One young nurse injected around my belly button, stated she couldn't look, withdrew the needle and stabbed me again.

After I received the initial two shots, I'd had enough of being a pin cushion for student nurses, so we returned to the mission, where Dad administered the remaining twelve shots.

He was scared and weary. But he said, in his later life, "At no time did we say, 'Let's quit. Let's go back to the States.' We had answered the call to serve."

Despite the laundry list of threats to our existence, there was never an offer from his medical colleagues inquiring whether he needed help or relief. Central Africa Mission continued to provide no solace or comfort. But we were fiercely independent. At last, the mission was taking on energy. It looked as if the new location had been the right decision after all.

During this time, Dad had established nine churches throughout the tribal trust area. He conducted a training class for African preachers once a week. He helped them with sermon preparation, and they would practice with one another in class. Mum prepared all the Sunday school materials and Bible stories for all the children at each church site. She painstakingly transformed the Caucasian features of Biblical characters into ones the African children could identify with.

On Sunday and Wednesday afternoons, she taught sewing to the women. During her monthly trips to Bulawayo, she purchased fabric and brought it back to the bush. The women loved bold colors, particularly with bright flowers, and she made sure she catered to their tastes. She began teaching them to make head scarves, then aprons, and next full skirts and then dresses. The people loved her. And she them.

One of the humorous side stories from the sewing classes was the circuitous routes of the exchange of money. We normally employed 20 workers at the mission. Every Monday, they received a week's ration of *mealie* meal, meat, veggies and slices of Sunlight soap. It

MISSION SITE NUMBER 2

was not unusual that, by Wednesday, the food was stolen by a fellow worker or traded.

This created enormous problems because now they were without food. On more than one occasion, there would be an ax-throwing fight because of the stealing, resulting in the need for stitches in heads in the middle of the night.

These activities became a little old, so once again my parents were creative. On one trip to town, we visited the bank and returned with bags of shiny new half-crowns (25 cents each). We stopped the weekly distribution of food, allowing the workers to be responsible for their rations. There was never a problem with middle-of-the-night fights after that. But Mum had several prostitutes in her sewing class. When they would purchase their sewing fabric from her, shiny coins would be dropped in Mum's hand.

We called that local circulation.

African children were being named after Mum. However, when the parents had heard Dad call Mum by her name—Fran—they had thought he was calling her "friend."

We never corrected them.

The men and women saw how Dad treated Mum. They witnessed his shows of respect. For instance, instead of walking five paces behind men, as was the custom for African women, Mum always walked in front of Dad. She also shared her knowledge of nutrition, farming, and gardening with the women and worked tirelessly in her own garden, sharing seeds and starters with the locals so they could begin producing healthy veggies and fruits themselves.

7
LOSING MISSION NUMBER 2

One afternoon, while Mum was working in the garden, she heard the sound of a helicopter. She looked up anxiously to see where it was going to land, but instead of landing, the pilot dropped a large envelope and she opened it.

The letter, printed on government stationery, said, "Stop building immediately." The government was planning on building a dam, which would result in the mission's being 30 feet underwater. Mum sank to the ground crying. The letter further stated there would be no compensation by the government for the buildings that would have to be abandoned.

We all ran to her and Dad cradled her in his arms. The family had been through so much already, and yet we'd been set up again. Unknown to us, Alan Wright, the district commissioner, a devout Catholic (who was in support of having a Catholic run mission), had known all along of the plans for the dam—built on the site he had fully endorsed and recommended we move to.

Although we did not receive any help or support from the other missionaries at Central Africa Mission, Dad continued to attend the quarterly meetings. Initially, he attended these meetings after traveling great distances. He hoped to commune with other missionaries and exchange ideas.

HOTDOGS FOR HYENAS

Most of the destinations had homes with wide, screened verandas, guesthouses, or nearby hotels for accommodations. Meals were catered. Dad went with the intention of rolling up his sleeves and working, but the others considered these meetings to be vacation time. He dryly observed that most of them were on vacation already.

Eventually, my parents felt there was too much empire-building by two of the head missionaries. Instead of bringing Africans to a better understanding of eternal salvation, he thought, these missionaries displayed greed, although they allegedly served the same God as he. He ruffled feathers at meetings by speaking out against other medical missionaries who declared Africans genetically deficient.

I became aware of the tenuousness of my parents' relationship with other missionaries during a quarterly mission meeting held in 1964 in the newly formed country of Zambia (formerly Northern Rhodesia). All of us mission kids were playing on the spectacularly manicured lawn of a hotel outside of the capital of Lusaka. As was typical, the men gathered for conferences while the women socialized. Mum wasn't the coffee klatch type although she walked around with a cup of black coffee in a green cup most of the time.

My most favorite friend, Alan, his brother David, and I were sitting on the freshly waxed red concrete floor of the hotel veranda just outside French doors that had been thrown open to let the fresh air seep into the conference room where our fathers were meeting. I could see Dad and two other prominently known missionaries in deep discussion.

One of them said, "Tom, Tom now listen, you must come to terms that they have genetic deficiencies."

Dad took command of the conversation with his booming voice. "I disagree. Show me the proof. You don't know what you're talking about." And with that he turned his muscular body sideways, strode through the French doors and looked down to where I was playing. He reached for my hand and nearly swept me off the ground. I had to jog alongside him to keep up with his long stride.

"I guess you heard some of that PK?" he said as we made our

LOSING MISSION NUMBER 2

way to find mother. I wasn't sure exactly what he was talking about, but I knew he was hot under the collar. I'd overheard Mum telling him to be wary of some of the missionaries, and he generally listened to her wise counsel. Dad was not going to be bullied — not by anyone. He was sufficiently angry to proclaim that we wouldn't join everyone for the luncheon that followed.

I was disappointed. The menus were handed out by waiters in starched white uniforms with burgundy and black fezes balanced on their heads. When they walked, the black fringe would sway back and forth from the top of their caps. You could go through the entire menu and then go back and repeat the courses you liked. Lamb curry and rice was my favorite. Plus, there was a never-ending supply of Coca Cola in glass bottles.

Mum changed gears and quickly made sandwiches and Dad continued ranting. "Genetic deficiencies? Hog wash! Compared to what? We will produce teachers, ministers and yes, doctors and nurses. Missionaries are not going to be here forever spooning out pablum."

Even at my tender age, I realized that my parents were dedicating their lives to sustainable outcomes. They were not going to ride the coattails of mission programs and retire into the sunset in some missionary retirement home basking in their wonderful accomplishments where other residents would never question their true contributions. Dad said that some of them could not get jobs as a "dog catcher" in America but ruled as monarchs on the mission field without being held accountable.

Our entire family found it unsettling when one of the wives of the "empire builders" bluntly told Mum and Dad at the mission meeting she would be designing the medical facility at Nuanetsi, even though she had never even come to visit the mission.

Dad was distraught. Mum, ever the helpmate, told him to watch his back and be careful of his comments. At the last night of the meeting, he stood in front of his fellow missionaries and told them the heartbreaking news about losing the second mission site.

To compound the anguish of relocating the mission, we discovered that District Commissioner Wright had made a *faux pas* that had created dissension and mistrust among Africans toward the Europeans regarding Maranda Tribal Trust Land. He had begun a project of building over a hundred small earth dams (such as the one at the first mission site at Melelzi), ranging in capacity from two hundred thousand to about a million and a half gallons. Wright had scheduled five major dams to be constructed later — one of which had been predetermined to be located at mission site number two.

The placement of the dams was intentional — with the goal of relocating sections of the Maranda population to the new small-dam areas. It was the opinion of the engineers and technical personnel that the dams would provide adequate permanent water for the population. However, the dams proved to be unreliable in the dry months because of their dependency on runoff to keep the water capacity at a level to meet the needs of the population.

Shortly after the completion of the small dams, Wright invited a group of European farmers to tour Maranda Tribal Trust Land and study the proposed major dam site at the confluence of the Nuanetsi and Dine Rivers. He claimed he'd received the blessing of Chief Maranda before taking a party of thirty farmers and ranchers on a tour of the tribal area, inspecting some twenty small dams and the magnificent, proposed site at the confluence of the two rivers.

Shortly after this tour, the government intelligence network reported that great numbers of tribesmen were joining the nationalist ranks in the hope that the nationalist leader would be able to stop the district commissioner from cutting up the Maranda tribal area into farms and giving them to Europeans. The tribesmen were convinced that Wright had spent large sums of money on five large dams and scores of small ones only because the area was to revert to its status under control of the old British Crown. Once the dams were built, the land would be allocated to European farmers who had already been taken around the area — by Wright himself — so that they could select their future farms.

LOSING MISSION NUMBER 2

We had not known that the "tour" had taken place. Nor were we aware of the feelings of the Africans in Maranda Tribal Trust Land regarding the fear of land removal. The average African had, out of necessity, become an absolute virtuoso in the art of disguising his or her true feelings when talking to strangers, particularly Europeans. Not even Dad was privy to the true thoughts of those he deemed his friends, but was instead told what they thought he wanted to hear.

Normally, tribal discussions of importance were held under a *ndaba* (discussion) tree. Tribesman would walk great distances to gather for a *ndaba* that would last from sunup to sundown. Dad was finally invited to attend one such meeting. It was there he learned that the building of the dam that would place the mission under water had been planned for a couple of years.

Because Dad was a European, the people of Maranda had assumed that he knew about the building of the dam and asked him whether he was part of the portioning of land to European farmers. He, of course, told them no. He had worked diligently to develop trust between himself and the people and as he spoke to them, he painfully shared his disappointment in what they had witnessed.

That particular *ndaba* and the invitation to Dad to attend was fortuitous, as the people were able to see his commitment to them. His relationship with the district commissioner, however, was forever damaged.

8
MISSION SITE NUMBER 3

At the third mission site, we were finally able to design the home the family had longed for. Dad had garnered sufficient American support to fund the mission and staff—and we were not going to capitulate. We had started over twice before and this iteration would be even more substantial.

We all had input into our first real home. I had an Etch-A-Sketch (one of the few toys we took to Africa) and had spent several years in serious design, creating my architectural wonder. I'm sure my home designs were impractical, but my parents did use my U-shaped cre-

ation. Dad built our four-bedroom home with a fireplace, a terraced backyard, and a formal dining room replete with French doors that opened onto a wide veranda between shade trees.

As the new house was being built, my pet Vervet monkey, Gi-Gi, would scamper up and down the unfinished walls, enjoying this new playground. Gi-Gi had been handed over to me as a baby by an Italian surveyor. His dogs had killed Gi-Gi's mother. When bored, Gi-Gi would sit on the outside of the windows and chew the putty off. We'd soften the putty with water and smooth over Gi-Gi's built-in teething ring with a putty knife, but days later, he'd be back at it again.

On one occasion, Gi-Gi decided to join us for dinner outdoors. He dropped off a nearby branch of the shade tree and landed straight in the bowl of gravy. After that, I had to put him up during meals. He loved grooming my horse and would pick nits—real or imaginary—off her mane as she moved around the yard.

Gi-Gi fell into discord with my mother on more than one occasion. Mum was a wonderful seamstress and rarely bought her dresses "off the rack." She had returned from teaching a women's sewing class on a Sunday afternoon and we were helping her unload the bolts of material, asking her how her day had been.

She was wearing a sun dress with a full skirt; the back had a very stylish round cut out. Gi-Gi kept jumping on her shoulder, wanting to be acknowledged, but she ignored him. He tried nibbling her black hair. No response. He stroked her ear. Still nothing. He jumped to her other shoulder and she continued chatting with us. Finally, in desperation for attention, my monkey toddler took action—he pooped down the cut-out in her dress.

Mum grabbed Gi-Gi's tail and flung him upwards. Disgusted, she headed straight in for the shower. Dad said, "Your mommy just put the first African monkey into orbit." We were nearly uncontrollable with laughter.

My parents' small office building, an aircraft hangar, and an enclosed shop were all close by. Dad created his own cinder blocks from a mold and concrete he manufactured locally. He had designed the mission site to be functional as well as secure. A wide grass runway divided the public clinic and schools from the private housing area.

Sanctions from the United Nations continued to cause a hiccup in getting supplies from the United States. Dad and I flew needed medical supplies from Johannesburg, South Africa. My parents began to accumulate dedicated clinical nursing staff. They eventually found a surgery supervisor, who hailed from Los Angeles.

MISSION SITE NUMBER 3

Nurse Marilyn Files's arrival was a turning point. She stood an imposing five feet eleven, weighed just north of two hundred pounds, and was used to having her way. She had expected to find the clinic equipped with a pristine Shampaine operating table like the ones in many of the well-funded African clinics she had researched. Considering the primitive conditions in the remote bush, however, an extravagant, state-of-the-art operating table was out of the question. Dad immediately redirected Nurse Files for a full year's training at neighboring Bulawayo's Mpilo Hospital to become certified as a midwife and immerse herself in Shona language and cultural terminology.

The Central Africa Mission began to push back, saying we had to hire African nurses from their local training program. But Dad expected the best African nursing staff and what he found at the Central Africa Mission's training program were inexperienced nurses with little ambition and less-than-ideal levels of commitment.

He decided to look at other options and visited the nursing program run by the Church of Sweden missions. The Manini mission was twenty minutes by air. The hospital and nursing school were beautifully laid out. Despite being of different denominations, the two missions shared the same commitment to compassionate outreach. Once established, it was a relationship that would span a decade.

Flying Mum and Nurse Marilyn Files to Swedish mission.

Our first African nurse, Roda, came from that program and brought a culture of trust and esteem essential to the longevity of the model. This further infuriated the Central Africa Mission empire builders. (Roda, by the way, stayed at the clinic for forty years.)

Admittedly, Dad was not being a team player. He was far more determined to create a sustainable, locally scalable Christian mission that changed lives — not to give glory limited to the upper echelon of Central Africa Mission.

Fast forward six months. The new (third) clinic at Nuanetsi was finally functioning. On opening day, 620 patients gathered on the front porch and across the swept-dirt yard (so designed so that intruding snakes could be easily seen and killed) to receive treatment. There was an examination room, surgery, a delivery suite, a lab, an x-ray, and four concrete huts outside for longer-term care of inpatients. Outside each hut was a cooking facility where patients could prepare their own food. Water and electricity were supplied by the main mission center.

620 patients gathered in the yard and in outpatient huts on opening day.

Dad continued studying and incorporating local African culture in our work. One change he made was to begin charging for the delivery of twins. In the local culture, it was believed that a woman

MISSION SITE NUMBER 3

could not give birth to two babies by one man — she had to have been unfaithful. When the twins were somewhere around the age of five months, the mother had to take a "journey" and come back with only one child. This happened even in cases of identical twins.

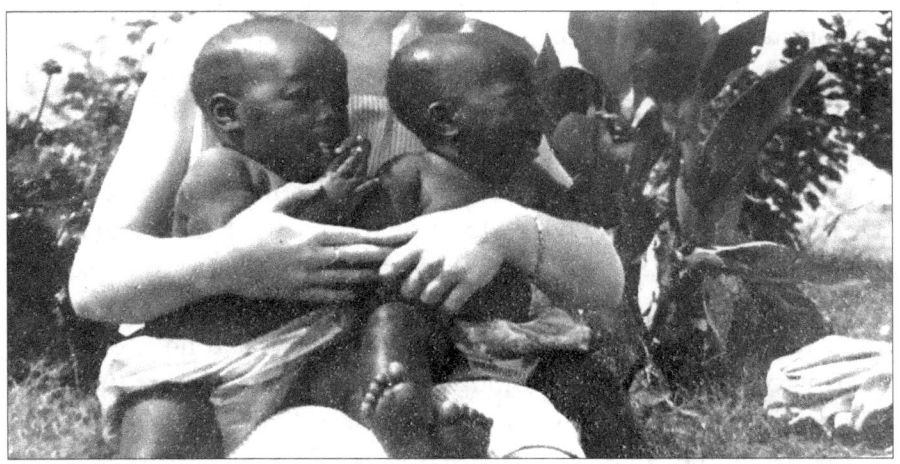

Me holding identical twins who didn't make it. Shortly after this photo was taken, the boys went on a "journey" with their mother. Only one returned with her.

Where women and children were chattel in our area, payment for twins became viewed as an investment. Children in Rhodesia/Zimbabwe were and continue to be the most vulnerable in the world. Caring for children who survived to age two was a perilous journey to begin with. Children did well while being breast fed, but once the next baby arrived, the outlook for the weaned child was dire. Over 25% of children under the age of five suffer stunted growth with nearly 10% severely stunted because of poor nutrition. Our local families needed educated support instead of outrage towards a practice of extinguishing the life of an infant twin. The charging for the delivery of twins now placed these saved children in a valued position. The average income for Africans was approximately $100 per year. My parents felt the only solution might be to ascribe a value to each child. As Dad had hoped, charging three dollars for a twin delivery improved the survival rate among twins.

In addition to charging for deliveries, we wanted to educate the African community on just how twins were conceived. Dad ordered reel-to-reel 16-millimeter films from Bulawayo and invited the local villages to the mission for a movie night. Using the back wall of the hangar for a projection screen, he set the projector up on scaffolding and started the generator. In the pristine darkness of the African night, the people began to arrive. They quickly filled up the entire floor of the hangar. Still more people came, and they spilled out onto the runway. Mum served popcorn and Kool-Aid.

Because the film was in English, our medical staff previewed the film several times. They stood at the front of the hangar and interpreted in the Shona language—an ingenious compromise that achieved the effect of subtitles. Over 250 people attended the film fest. They wanted to see it again and again. Dad had helped change their perception of twins without once telling the villagers that their practice of destroying a twin was wrong.

By 1967, the mission construction was deemed complete. All basic essentials were functioning, the buildings were attractively laid out, and the clinic was operating at maximum capacity.

Dad replaced the Cessna 180 with a six-seat, high-performance, turbocharged Cessna 206. Its double cargo doors alongside the fuselage allowed easy access to get a patient on a stretcher into and out of the aircraft.

The mission's reach expanded to sixteen churches and a successful divinity school for African preachers. The primary schools were also flourishing. For school stability, we hired husband-and-wife teaching teams. The students wore school uniforms. If they couldn't afford the costs, we covered it. Fabric for the school uniforms was bussed in, a tailor with a treadle sewing machine set up shop, and the uniforms were locally made.

To establish community pride and develop entrepreneurial skills, we built a store close to the mission, run by the local tribe.

MISSION SITE NUMBER 3

Problems Escalate

In contrast to their long habit of marginalization of our efforts, the Central Africa Mission decided our rapidly-evolving third mission complex would be a prime location to hold one of their regular quarterly meetings. Despite the fact that none of them had ever set foot on any of the Maranda Tribal Trust sites, in May, fifty missionaries descended on our recently carved-out paradise. Mum, who was so proud of having a beautiful home, was visibly upset when unsupervised children kicked her new and freshly painted walls.

Shortly after this wonderful "convention" of the regional missions, my family's problems escalated. Central Africa Mission demanded that nurses from America begin rotations between the various mission sites. Shocked by the immense impact of our low-budget, self-sufficient, fiercely independent team, the organization now wanted credit for our progress and they wanted to integrate and control operations with the system at large. Central Africa Mission wanted to capitalize on the knowledge and expertise of our Nurse Files. They wanted their nurses to experience working in the highly successful and well-respected Nuanetsi clinic. Suddenly, our clinic was a model to be replicated.

Fifty missionaries gathered at our newly constructed home in the bush.

But Dad said no. Nurse Files had no desire or intention of being shipped to other medical mission sites. She had raised her own travel funds and financial support to work with us at Nuanetsi. Her benefactors in the United States backed her. The staff and patients at Nuanetsi loved her.

Next, Central Africa Mission wanted another doctor to fly in on

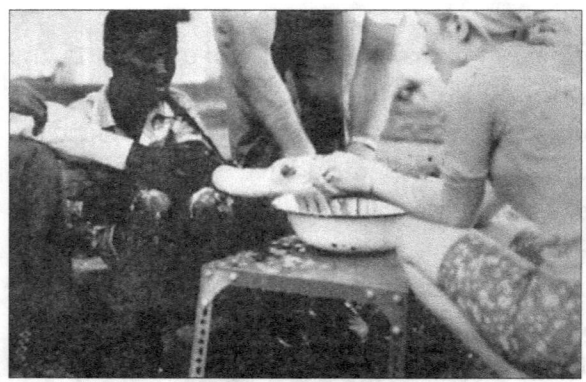
Me helping set a broken arm in the bush.

a weekly basis to observe how the clinic operated, to learn how it had penetrated the region so effectively, and to "lend a hand" when needed.

Again, Dad said no. The doctor pushing this agenda was one of the "power players" who had contributed to the foundation of the main regional hospital a few hours away. Although he was also a pilot, he had never flown to or visited our mission, and was the very same man who had declined to send help to Dad during those early years at the first two mission sites, even when my father had expressed dire need.

In contrast, our relationship with the Swedish mission flourished. Our mission began a delightful and engaging partnership with a Dr. Olle, a native of Stockholm. Dr. Olle was a pilot, dentist, and medical doctor who had left his wife and children in Sweden to serve in Rhodesia. He flew into our clinic once a week, attended to all dental needs, stayed for lunch, and flew out any patients who needed to be treated at his hospital.

It was a relationship that ran very smoothly. Dr. Olle was slightly built with light hair and a breezy personality, talked a mile a minute, and appeared to be a full-speed-ahead cowboy type. There were times he caused us anxiety with his take-offs. Instead of taxiing down the end of the runway and using the full length of the airstrip, he often started the takeoff roll where he parked, right in front of the hangar. This was the midway point, so he only had half the runway. There was no margin for error. The slightest mechanical hiccup would doom a departure. But Dr. Olle loved life and patients loved him.

MISSION SITE NUMBER 3

Several years later, I visited him and his family at their home in Sweden and he invited me to go to his clinic with him in Stockholm. I imagined his very established and austere patients would have been astounded to learn what he accomplished in Africa. Both he and my family were committed to helping the locals, but more than acute care, they wanted to provide the resources to educate the local people on how to diagnose and treat common ailments.

News of our successful expansion reached the ears of the power brokers of Central Africa Mission. In addition, Dad developed the respect of both the white and black communities. After years of disappointment, he was creating a model that worked.

This result infuriated the two influential Central Africa Mission leaders. They repeatedly and pointedly reminded Dad he was under *their* umbrella, not Sweden's. They demanded that my family and all missionaries under the Central Africa Mission umbrella to pay the organization 20 percent of their income to cover their administrative overhead. They also claimed that the aircraft and vehicles owned by my parents were theirs. The absurdity over that claim was unconscionable.

More and more mission families were coming to Rhodesia, but they were going to the cities or established mission stations. No new areas were being carved out. In reality, the money they were demanding would be syphoned into the pockets of the power brokers.

Dad pushed back. He believed he was the voice that spoke on behalf of all missionaries. He made the extreme step of declaring his mission as autonomous. He flew to the United States and spoke to all his supporting churches. The churches and his own personal board signed affidavits supporting my parents and their unique style of mission operation. It was not their intention that their mission support benefit other missions.

In response, the Central Africa Mission decided to play hardball. They sued Dad in U.S. courts, declaring that my parents' aircraft, vehicles, buildings, and equipment all belonged to the organization. My parents were stunned. This was their personal property.

Mum and Dad flew to the United States to defend their position and the case was thrown out of court. But Dad's position was further undermined when all the other missionaries under the umbrella voted to contribute their assets and then to redirect 20 percent of future donations toward supporting the "premier" Christian mission organization (Central Africa Mission).

Dad was now an outlier. However, the other missions did not have the long commitments and great financial investment my parents had personally secured. The other missions had moved either into already constructed, funded, and functioning missions or into urban centers not requiring substantial infrastructure support. They did not have to design water or electric systems and build roads, schools, clinics, and homes.

Central Africa Mission next moved their legal attacks from America, where the predominant financial support was underwritten, to the local courts in Rhodesia. In the complaint, they declared that the organization owned the mission, even the house my family had built and paid for. Dad again fought for what he believed was right. He retained a well-respected law firm from Bulawayo. For the attorneys to understand the function of our mission, they flew in on several occasions to see the lay of the land. Our lawyers countersued in the local high court. The battle lines were clearly drawn, and the legal wrangling lasted six years. Central Africa Mission outmaneuvered and far outspent my parents in the legal skirmishes. After his initial defeat, Dad appealed to the government and he was granted a stay.

Despite the personal turmoil, Dad continued to be respected among the Africans he was serving. At Christmas, we introduced Christmas caroling. Loading members of the church in the back of our truck, we drove through the winding bush roads, singing carols in the Shona language and sharing the songs in the villages where they stopped.

"We realized that one day there would be no more missionaries," Dad said. "The young locally-recruited and trained preachers could all read and write. I insisted upon that; however, we had expositories. These older men had the respect of the community. The younger

MISSION SITE NUMBER 3

preachers would read from the Scripture and then preach. The expository would stand next to him, explaining in great detail what the Scripture really meant to the people. The older person had the cultural credibility and the voice of authority."

During Sunday service, more of them answered the invitational call for baptism. Immediately following the service, they would sing in harmony as they walked to the nearest river or water hole to be baptized. The African preachers were now baptizing their own people. It was such a joy to see this growth. Dad would stand on the bank to greet them as they would emerge from the water. He would then look above to where I was standing and give me a wink. During most of the baptismal services, I stood quietly with a Winchester .30-30 trained on a crocodile that could have easily disrupted the service.

The Africans' understanding of the second coming of Christ was deeply spiritual. When one of the elders of a nearby village was dying, he made a special request of us. He wanted to be buried sitting up so he could be the first one to jump up and greet Jesus when he came again. After the old man's passing, we helped dig out an earthen bench in the side of an old anthill. We carefully placed the body in a seated position before filling the grave with dirt.

Challenges Continue

During this time, my parents recruited another family to join us at the mission. The father of the family was a Federal Aviation Administration–certified airframe and power plant (A&P) mechanic, but my parents did not thoroughly review all his credentials by obtaining references from the airport where the mechanic had last worked. (Years later, my brother found his credentials to be less than stellar.) Soon after the new missionary arrived, Dad asked him to adjust the timing of his turbocharged Cessna 206.

When the job was completed, Dad flew the one hour to Bulawayo. Midflight, he began having difficulty with the aircraft's powerplant. Upon emergency landing, he found a cotter pin had been left out and had become lodged between the magnetos. Fortunately, there are two sets of magnetos, so the engine performance was only slightly diminished. His usual aircraft mechanic counseled him, chiding him for not fully investigating the man he had allowed to work on the aircraft.

Dad flew back to the mission, furious. Because everyone in our family flew in that aircraft, safety was always his top priority. He spoke to the new missionary-cum-mechanic and found he had not performed the mandatory cotter-pin count during completion of maintenance.

Dad's vehement admonishment eventually came back to haunt him. Revenge came late, but loud. The Central Africa Mission discovered they had an inside discontent in the new recruit and enlisted his help by promising that he would be able to run the entire mission if he could cast doubt, both stateside and in the African country, regarding Dad. Now that the hard work of establishing a functioning facility was done, they still wanted to appropriate the mission and credit.

It didn't take long for the requested information to flow surreptitiously back to Central Africa Mission. The relationship with the organization continued to be a high-wire act with chain saws. We were battling Central Africa Mission while our adopted country was also in a battle against terrorism.

In light of what had happened in Kenya during the Mau Mau uprising nearly twenty years before, Rhodesia wanted to avoid a repeat of the slaughter of missionaries and farmers living in isolated areas. In Kenya, underground political meetings, where terrorists plotted to kill those who were helping support, feed, and maintain the country, took place in the shadows at night. Included in these rituals was the drinking of blood. Not wanting to repeat history, the Rhodesian government ordered that no nighttime meetings could take place in the schools. We suspected that one of our schoolteachers who was not from the area was involved in conducting these night-time terrorist training sessions.

"I knew for my own personal safety," Dad said, "that it would not be wise to simply walk into the school building at night. I waited

MISSION SITE NUMBER 3

for a moonless night and slipped on dark coveralls. I waited for the meeting to break up. It wasn't long, and I could see the teacher exit the building. I had already warned him, for the increased security and safety of others, to use the gate at night before crossing the airfield to the temporary teachers' housing. He was defiant and continued to slip through the fence. As the teacher unknowingly approached me, he separated the strands of the eight-gauge wire fence and stooped through the opening. I cocked my Colt .45 by his ear.

"*Madagwani*, good evening," I said.

For the second time, Dad had stopped a teacher from bringing harm to the peaceful community. As you may remember, the first teacher had stolen the schoolchildren's government-issued dried food, and now this firebrand was encouraging subversive activities among the local tribesmen.

Dad drove the teacher to the police station at Nuanetsi, forty miles away. He was informed by the chief of police that intelligence had already reported the teacher as a terrorist intending to bring harm to the mission. Unfortunately, that information was not forwarded to our supporters in America. Members of Central Africa Mission fanned the flame with stateside supporters, claiming that "Tom Courtney was out of control, pulling a gun on an African who was sharing the Gospel with others."

Next, Central Africa Mission filed a court action in Rhodesia stating that Dad could not resign from their organization as he claimed to have done because he had willingly come to Africa under their umbrella. Members of the organization made trips to the United States in an attempt to undermine us and our work. They searched for anyone Dad had crossed during his career, and they found a few who were willing to speak against him.

This band of discontents made enough waves that churches began to withdraw financial support. They didn't want to be placed in the middle of such glaring disharmony. But Senator Barry Goldwater, a personal friend of Dad's, and Oregon governor Mark Hatfield, a former classmate, went to bat for him stateside. They spoke on Dad's behalf, reiterating that no one was more competent, qualified, or selfless, that no one had the passion, dedication, and vision he brought to Africa.

In retaliation for this new momentum of support, Central Africa Mission then submitted court documents stating that Dad had physically abused Africans. They positioned themselves in a convoluted attack supported with untruths. He appealed and requested a meeting with his accusers in court. This request was denied. Central Africa Mission sought and received a continuance.

A few months later, the power brokers of Central Africa Mission agreed to meet Dad in Fort Victoria, 140 miles away, behind closed doors. He went in hopes that they would leave him alone to operate the mission in peace. But once the doors closed at the meeting, it was evident their intention was not peaceful, nor were they going to relent. In addition, they told him he must repent before them.

He left the meeting in tears. He made another last-ditch emergency trip to the United States, defending his right to run his mission without interference. His funding dwindled, yet he was committed to operating the mission.

Dad accepted several income-generating positions both privately and within the government, piloting executives and officials into and out of the country. This critical lifeline kept the clinic and mission financially solvent.

In addition, sanctions still plagued the country. Supplies, especially technical components, were difficult to obtain. Dad needed a lens for a microscope and a part for the turboprop of the 206. Each time, the parts would be sent from the United States through Great Britain. Each time, Great Britain would return the boxes as soon as they saw the destination was Rhodesia. (Great Britain did not want any equipment to enter Rhodesia that could benefit the industry or the well-being of the country.) On the third attempted shipment, Dad requested that the parts be listed as a coffee pot for personal use. The lens and aircraft parts shipped straight through.

Despite the continued mission controversy, Mum continued to teach the African women. Then, while preparing to leave one

MISSION SITE NUMBER 3

Mum cared for the needs of others before her own.

day for a sewing class in the bush fifteen miles away, she became ill. Dad attempted to persuade her to stay, but she insisted that the women were waiting for her. Before leaving, however, she agreed to be tested for bilharzia.

When she returned to the mission, she stopped by the clinic to check on the test results but found Dad and the staff in the middle of a very difficult delivery of twins. One twin was born alive, the other fetus and the mother were in distress. Mum's typical selfless persona went into overdrive. She summarily waived the need to know her test results and jumped in to help. Mum loaded the mother into the Land Rover to take her to the aircraft so we could take the mother to a larger medical facility. Everyone knew better than to insist Mum stay behind—despite looking like death, this small soft-spoken woman had the tenacity and courage of a lioness.

During takeoff, Mum knelt beside the young mother, keeping her calm. Once aloft, I heard Mum say to the mother, "Sundai" (meaning, "Push"). The dead fetus was delivered, followed by the placenta. Once they landed in Bulawayo, Mum and I escorted the mother and the surviving twin to Mpilo Hospital, ten miles away, leaving Dad to clean up the aircraft. It was only after the admission process was complete and we returned that Mum asked Dad what her test results had been. She had bilharzia, he said, and was gravely ill.

We returned to the mission to begin her intensive treatment. The house became exceedingly quiet. The curtains in the bedroom remained closed. I was afraid to enter the bedroom, as I'd never seen my mother so ill that she was unable to rise from her bed. The use of Miracil D (or

Nilodin) was the common treatment for these nasty parasites and the treatment was often considered worse than the disease.

This was the first time a member of our family had contracted bilharzia. Giddiness, diarrhea, vomiting, tremors, and neurological manifestations from the treatment were common. Often patients would see doors and trees moving away as they walked toward them, and then they'd feel they were colliding with the objects.

Mum experienced all these adverse effects. She could barely eat. She couldn't walk unassisted. She felt as if she were climbing the corner of the wall in the bedroom. It was two weeks before she fully recovered.

Soon after the bilharzia episode, Mum was back to her gardening. She normally kept the gate shut to keep the dogs out of the beds, but one day she forgot—and it turned out to be divine providence. My Doberman, Dobie, darted through the gate and grabbed a cobra that was inches from Mum, killing it within seconds.

A few weeks later, while Dad was flying clients to Mozambique, Dobie once again discovered a cobra on the front lawn, but this time, though she fought valiantly, the dog was struck by the cobra and died. Mum radioed Dad—he wanted to return immediately to comfort us but flying over the bush at nightfall was difficult. He did not want us to have to put lanterns on the runway or drive vehicles out across the threshold so he could identify the airstrip. He was forced to let us grieve alone while he performed ferry missions to keep hope alive.

The six-year legal battle with Central Africa Mission continued to spin out of control. On his way to one of the many court hearings, in the capital city of Salisbury (now Harare), Dad was stopped by security as he entered the airport. After landing and receiving instructions from the tower, he always parked, checked the aircraft, and left directions for refueling the Cessna 206. He entered the same gate he had been in and out of for nine years.

When Dad entered the terminal this time, the security guard asked to see his pilot's license. This was the usual procedure. Customarily,

MISSION SITE NUMBER 3

Dad would chat with security as they checked his credentials. They would typically converse with him casually in their native Shona, and he knew most of them by first name. On this particular trip, though, he didn't recognize the guard on duty. After asking for the appropriate identification, the guard immediately reported to the authorities that Dad had been abusive toward him. Dad became alarmed when he overheard the guard speaking in ominous tones that reeked of a personal vendetta. The new guard was unaware that Dad spoke fluent Shona.

Subsequently, Dad was arrested. The guard stated in the magistrate's court that Dad had said, "Don't touch my license with your dirty black hands." The guard claimed he had been called an "animal, a baboon, and a stupid little creature."

Dad argued that this had never happened, stating that his organization contributed over $50,000 a year in direct funding and countless volunteer hours toward African education, and he certainly would not use such an expression. (The word "creature" would not have been used by a European let alone an American.)

The state alleged that Dad had refused to allow the airport guard to examine his license, wouldn't give his name and address to the sergeant of the Department of Civil Aviation, and entered the airport through a restricted gate. The magistrate said the court found that the state witnesses could be relied on and discounted Dad's suggestion that the security guards had been "schooled" in their evidence. Dad was found guilty of failing to comply with directions for regulating his movements and conduct given by an authorized officer within a protected area. He was fined.

The government-run newspaper found this insignificant piece of news to be worthy of front-page prominence.

9
LOSING MISSION NUMBER 3

We knew Central Africa Mission had carefully orchestrated the administrative confrontation and subsequent press coverage. The organization, in their plot to take over our mission, was intransigent. They had not been successful in their effort to plant evidence that Dad was abusive toward Africans, but now they had what they needed to drive a wedge between Dad and the government officials he had developed respectable relationships with. Central Africa Mission was willing to pay any price to force him out of Africa.

Eventually, Central Africa Mission would win their case against Dad. The government simply could not ignore the accusation that Dad was "abusive" toward the people he was serving. Government officials had received enough money to make it worthwhile to rule against him. They had little to lose in ousting one white missionary.

Dad could not afford, nor did he have the fortitude, to continue this protracted battle — first within the organization and then through the courts. How much more pain did this organization intend to inflict on him, his family and his work? The answer would soon come. Within a couple of months, the Rhodesian government declared Dad *persona non grata.*

Mum was not forced to leave the country. Central Africa Mission allegedly wanted to "spare" her, but they knew she would not stay and run the mission without Dad.

Central Africa Mission and its two greedy leaders were satisfied they could now comfortably take over this thriving mission and its bustling clinic. Dad was given limited time before he had to leave the country, leaving Mum alone at the mission to pack.

The African ministers and members of the sixteen established churches gathered at the mission. The schoolchildren and teachers, *kraal* heads, the very elderly Chief Maranda, and the *nganga* came. They were losing the missionary and his family they loved and respected and considered one of their own. They began singing "God Be with You 'Till We Meet Again."

The singing turned into an evangelistic service. One by one the people of Maranda came forward and shared their testimony. The service lasted hours, ending with a call of dedication. Twenty people came forward to make a confession, asking to be baptized that very day in the Nuanetsi River. At the close of the service, the last hymn, "It Is Well with My Soul," was sung with tears streaming down everyone's face. Dad prayed that peace like a river would attend every one of them. The tears were the first step in an arduous healing process that persists to this day.

Neighboring white farmers came from as far as a hundred miles away to help, offering to store generators, welders, and other equipment at their farms. My parents accepted their generous offers. Mum began the arduous and difficult task of loading furniture onto the truck, taking it to the railway station and on to auction in South Africa.

Once at the railway station, she was stopped from loading all the furniture onto the train. The Rhodesian government mandated that only a one-bedroom suite could leave the country. The list of what could not leave the country seemed to grow daily and was becoming endless. She had the choice of abandoning the furniture or giving it away to rail employees.

Mum had to say goodbye to items she had helped build or accumulate over the years, including many of the furnishings we had constructed from scratch. She cried uncontrollably and with deep

LOSING MISSION NUMBER 3

anguish. The message was loud and clear: She felt she would never have a home again.

But my parents did find a home in neighboring Botswana, 200 miles from the mission and the move to Botswana provided time for beginning the healing process. They purchased a 10,000-acre farm just over the border. Their love of Africa was unshakable.

But the unthinkable happened. One of the Central Africa Mission's missionaries contacted me, sending me photos. The mission and our well-crafted home that they planned to slide into and take over had had some things removed! They were stunned. The home and buildings my family had built weren't as they remembered.

My dad had removed the steel-framed door, window frames, and other items that he had purchased with his own personal funds. These frames were stored by local farmers, and eventually found their way south to be reused.

Progressive Change

Of my family's two primary opponents within the Central Africa Mission, the main aggressor involved in taking the mission from us died in 1995; the other was still living in 2013. I decided to extend an olive branch to the surviving conspirator, with whom I had shared a special bond as a child. He'd nicknamed me "Goosey Gander," and I, initially oblivious to what he would ultimately do to my dad, idolized him. I located his medical practice in America, and was given his personal phone number. When I identified myself on the phone, a long, uncomfortable silence ensued—he had obviously never expected to hear from me. He apologized for his actions that had disrupted my life and destroyed my family's mission career.

After reconnecting, the two of us spent the next year in frequent contact until his untimely death from cancer. I attended his funeral in a gesture to further heal the wounds that existed between his family and me. My brother Michael thought I was stark raving mad and had no interest in mending fences, but this elderly physician and I had finally found "peace like a river."

HOTDOGS for HYENAS

A few years before my family made our exit from the African bush—in 1979—Michael made a commitment to return to Africa. While still in college, he and his bride spent a summer at our mission at Nuanetsi, working in the clinic and mission. Michael returned to the United States and graduated *magna cum laude*, while his wife completed nursing school. My brother and his young bride had long aspired to live and work in Africa, following the path of my parents. Michael was softer and less confrontational in personality than Dad, but although they stood toe-to-toe on more than one occasion, they respected each other and worked together well.

Michael wanted to begin with a more traditional missionary role in the field, and his wife was similarly committed to being a part of the medical mission team. After graduating from college, they decided to remain in the U.S. to settle into conventional careers and begin their family in the safer haven of America, but the passion for serving in Africa simmered beneath the surface.

After their second child turned two, the opportunity for them to return to Africa arose. They intended to join my parents, but it became increasingly clear that this was no longer prudent. Our parents were encountering escalating friction with Central Africa Mission.

Michael and his family could see that their longevity of service in that sector would be minimal and persistently disrupted because of the incessant lawsuits. The writing was on the wall. Central Africa Mission had no intention of allowing our initiative to succeed. The Mission passed its leadership from father to son while simultaneously precluding my family from enjoying the same legacy. In addition, the Bush War was still raging throughout Rhodesia (which was now several independent countries, including our area in what is now Zimbabwe). Maranda Tribal Trust Land (the extensive tract of land reserved by the government for settlement by indigenous black people) was a hotbed for terrorist activities and was becoming progressively more dangerous for both whites and blacks.

Now that Michael and his wife had children of their own, they felt the situation was even more unsuitable for raising a family. They

LOSING MISSION NUMBER 3

turned their sights north and west toward Kenya and Ethiopia, where they had close missionary friends who encouraged them to consider relocating. As they went through the process of readying themselves for the mission field, it gradually became clear that Kenya would be the preferable choice.

This decision turned out to be providential. If they had gone to Ethiopia, they would have arrived just in time to be banned by the government along with all the other missionaries, who were abruptly and violently deported. However, the doors to Kenya remained open.

Michael and his wife began to raise funds through the churches on the American West Coast, where they then resided. The denomination they were seeking support from had already been through the wringer with Central Africa Mission's vilifying our Dad. Central Africa Mission representatives had made numerous trips to these churches, "encouraging" them to discontinue support for the Courtney family.

What should have been an easy transition into a second generation committed to serving on the mission field was quite the contrary. When church board members and influential members of congregations realized Michael was the son of Tom Courtney, many doors were slammed in his face. Church supporters were afraid that the discord with Central Africa Mission would not stop and that the bureaucracy would focus on completing the destruction of my family's mission and the easy solution for the local American churches would be to refuse even modest support to Michael.

This further reinforced how much Central Africa Mission continued to resent the tremendous progress that my family had achieved in our work in the African mission field. They resented my father's close relationship with the indigenous inhabitants and his acceptance of some of their customs as a means of solidifying the call to Christ.

But Michael, undeterred, pressed on and within six months obtained the commitments they needed to serve in Kenya. Michael had no interest in being a lone wolf like Dad. He truly wanted to be part of an integrated team but, like our parents, believed that a missionary should first be a good cultural anthropologist. He abhorred the practices of other missionaries who tried to cram American culture down the throats of African people and call it Christianity.

Having been raised on the mission field, he had carefully analyzed the biggest failures of missionaries. "[Because of] ethnocentrism and being so enamored with their own ideas and goals," he says, "many missionaries couldn't shut up and listen to what God was already doing in the African people's own culture. A tremendous amount of damage between missionaries and those they are called to serve is a direct result of the missionary's failure to prepare themselves in the realm of local cultural education."

Michael served six years in Kenya but never returned to Africa permanently as he had planned. Central Africa Mission, did not have a base in Kenya, but still attempted to disrupt Michael's service in Kenya by sending a second generation leader (near Mike's age) into the country, but this failed.

My brother confronted this controversy head on. A massive chunk of his youth and a significant portion of his young adulthood had been dedicated to the African people, but his continued role there was finished. My family, including my parents' two grandchildren (in total, all three generations) had served and sacrificed. At this point, there was personal satisfaction but precious little else to show for our sacrifices.

Today, many years later, I struggle to evaluate our collective impact. But, I've found that although doubt clouds our memories, answers to the questions still come. I recently received a message on Facebook, signed by someone who had known my family since her infancy. For her protection, even to this day, I withhold the name.

> Hi Pamela:
> I was born at Dine Mission clinic in 1974 with sister Mtimkulu as my midwife. My family homestead is about 8km from Dine. Dine now has got a high school which was built during the good

LOSING MISSION NUMBER 3

Zimbabwean old days. Now the mission school is a far cry from the old self. You can talk of cracked walls, fading paint works, a shortage of teachers, and a general decline of infrastructure at the once glamorous mission compound. I greatly appreciate the work of the missionaries during the Rhodesian era and I have no doubt that the majority of Zimbabweans today would vote for the return of Rhodesia in a referendum given the opportunity.

Then, in late 2020 at the South Africa Shop in Charlotte, North Carolina, I was standing in line to pay for homemade *boerewors* and imported foods from the country of South Africa. I began chatting with another customer. In the conversation, we acknowledged that most of the customers we saw were from South Africa.

I asked him where he was from. "Zimbabwe," he said. "Bulawayo, to be exact. Where are you from?"

"Nuanetsi. Wanezi," I replied.

His eyes became huge. "My brother went to school at Wanezi in 1980!"

When I told him my family had opened the school in 1967, he was absolutely stunned. What a celebration!

We *had* made a difference.

PART 3

Mum with a cobra she shot in my brother's bedroom. It had crawled in and gotten tangled up on a kite hanging on his wall. Bottom left of the photo is one of my faithful dachshunds.

10
MY FAVORITE SNAKE STORIES

Before my birth, my parents agonized over what given name would be suitable for me. Colleen and Pamela were the top runners and they both flowed well with the last name of Courtney.

Now for my middle name. The plan was for it to be Katherine, in honor of my grandmother who had emigrated to America as part of the persecuted Volga Germans. She and her family were part of the mass exodus from Norka, Russia at the beginning of the last century. Kate, as she was known, stood 4'10", was *pixyish*, wore size four shoes, was spunky, raised six children, and owned some of the largest apple orchards in Hood River, Oregon. But hanging the name of Katherine after Pamela seemed heavy and Kate just didn't go, so I became Pamela Kay.

My father always called me PK. Dad rather liked having a daughter who was known by her initials. In my first fledgling script as a four-year-old, I signed my name "PK Courtney." (I thought that was my proper name. The only time I heard Pamela Kay was when I was in deep doo-doo over something.)

Anyway, we were off to Africa. Destination: Cape Town, South Africa. While on board ship, I became aware that I wasn't the only important PK in the world. *Picune Kaya,* or PK, was the French-inspired common term used for "toilet" or "outhouse" in southern Africa. "Going to the PK" did not mean someone was going to visit me.

HOTDOGS FOR HYENAS

Within minutes of meeting my new young friends in Africa, they used the opportunity to make light of it. To my childhood friend and fellow MK (missionary kid), Alan Smith (now a refined pediatrician and still my endeared *boetie* from another mother), I was known as "PK Toilet." During my teens, my brother and his friends decided to shower me with what only a brother's friends could do. Another nickname: *boeremeisie* PK. *Boeremeisie* is Afrikaans for "farm girl." (I trust that you understand why my middle name never appeared on my college diplomas.)

During the early 1960s, we lived on top of a *kopje* (Afrikaans for rock outcropping). Four-wheel drive was the only way to get to this little piece of *potential* paradise. The weather was hot and dry—the only relief the occasional puff of air that would bounce up from the dam below. There were trees on top of the *kopje* for shade and my mother had gardens, but it was far from a Garden of Eden. To add a splash of color during severe droughts, Mum planted a few plastic flowers by the granite boulders that lined our rock patio. Our houseboy, Marata, showed me how to make paint by mixing fire ash with water. Instant bush artist. I painted the rocks, creating eye popping drama to Mum's plastic flowers.

One morning while hunting for rock rabbits—or *dassies* as we called them—on the other side of the *kopje*, my brother and I watched a robust-looking rock python warming himself in the morning sun close to where the *dassies* were running about. *Dassies* are quick and easy meals for pythons.

These prolifically-breeding "rodents" look much like overgrown guinea pigs. Curiously, their closest relatives are elephants. Often the animals are hunted and their pelts used to make a *kaross*, a bedcover to sleep under. Silvery brown in color, they scurry over rock ledges with their large families. They have rubber-like foot pads that allow them to literally "stick" to the sides of the rocks. Weighing in at around eight pounds, *dassies* are capable of making over 20 different noises. Usually, there is one family member who is a sentry, squealing out signals when danger comes close.

MY FAVORITE SNAKE STORIES

My brother Michael and I had been looking for the python for weeks. One of the African kids had been climbing around the rocks and this python had sunk its bacteria-laden teeth into his foot. His family had taken him to the local *nganga* (witch doctor) for treatment, but infection trumped the local *muti* (medicine) and the child lost his big toe. The tissue surrounding the big toe died, leaving the inside of his foot concave, a nearly perfect half-moon shape.

Mike motioned to me to stay perfectly still. I could hear him breathe in and hold his breath. Steady. He leveled the Winchester .30-30 to his shoulder and with open sights pulled the trigger. A clean shot drilled through the python's expansive head.

The *dassies* gave off a trilling noise, disappearing deep into little caves. Silence. I stood up and grinned.

"You got him. Jolly good show."

Mike took the sling of the rifle and moved his weapon around to his back. We climbed down from our rocky perch and headed towards the python. While the nine-foot serpent was still writhing and whipping around, we grabbed the hook of the tail and began running with it as fast as we could.

"Mum, Mum, look what we have," we yelled as we came close to the house. "Can we dissect him and see what he looks like inside?"

Dad had gone to town, 250 miles away, and Mum knew if he'd been there, he'd have been right in the middle of our spontaneous hands-on biology class. We decided our surgical table would be one of those beautifully painted rocks.

Mike proceeded to pull out his trusty knife. I said, "Don't use that—let's use some of the Bard-Parkers (surgical blades) from Dad's medical supplies." I was pretty confident he wouldn't mind. Especially if we didn't cut ourselves and, afterward, handed them back to Mum to be boiled for sterilization.

"Here PK," said my brother, "you help stretch the snake out on his back while I go get the blades."

Every time I thought I had the python stretched into submission, it would make a serpentine move and roll off the rock. I'd drag part of his body up, go down and get the rest of him, and start the process all over again. Before Mike could return with the blades, Marata, who never moved quickly, came strolling around the yard. He took one look at me with my new dangerous playmate and began screaming.

"Madame, Madame, a big snake has little *nkoskas* (little girl)."

He was deathly afraid of snakes. Mum looked up casually to see me wrangling the dead python. She was at the outdoor clothesline. Dad had fashioned wire hooks for her and she was twisting these hooks through six-inch strips of freshly killed kudu meat and hanging them on the clothesline to make *biltong* (Afrikaans for bull's tongue because of the way it looked). *Biltong* was our staple, our comfort food given our limited refrigeration. She barely responded to Marata. By then, he had already shinnied up a scrawny tree, the limb of which he was balancing on was bending low to the ground.

About that time, Mike appeared with the blades, handed me one, and together, we began slicing the belly of the snake from stem to stern. Marata, still convinced the snake was alive, began telling us how brave (or stupid) we were—to him, we had singlehandedly killed this monster-eating python with two little knives. (I don't think we ever told him any different.)

"Hey, Marata, come here, please." I said. I wanted to show him the orange-looking intestines I'd just found. To me this was better than discovering gold.

But Marata was having nothing to do with the innards of the snake. Normally, he loved to be in our photos, but declined to be in our family portrait with the snake. The next day when Marata arrived at work, he found we had skinned, salted and laid the snake out to dry. On our next trip to town, the snake would be going with us to the taxidermist.

Marata made a wide berth around the snakeskin, quietly mixed up some ash and water mixture, and freshened up our rock surgical suite.

Most of the time, life was pleasant up on the *kopje*, but at night, sometimes terrifying events would take place. The bookshelf near my school desk, for instance, held a couple of jars of scorpions. I had confiscated these large black nuisances from my *veldschoons* (Afrikaans for tan, suede shoes worn in the bushveld) where they had found comfort in the toes of my shoes during the night.

I don't really remember ever wearing the *veldschoons*, but we still shook out our shoes each morning. Wearing flip flops or being barefoot seemed a whole lot safer to us kids. I remember telling Dad one day, while we were walking through the bush, how safe I was for wearing my "vellies."

"Daddy," I said, "no snakes can bite me."

Dad smiled. "Honey, please remember that one can rear up and strike you in the body."

That made my decision easy. Just don't wear shoes.

We had a fine true PK (outhouse) on the *kopje*. From our rock patio, a trail led down the hill past the chicken coop which housed George (because he was the first chicken, a gift from a local village), Paul (my favorite), John and Ringo. A couple of my chickens became casualties of late-night mongoose marauders.

Torches (flashlights) were nice to have to light the way down the path but could never be depended upon. It wasn't fun to be shaking a torch up and down to get the last of the light drained out only to go completely dark. After all, there were snakes out there at night.

We used Tilly lanterns that Mum would fill every day for nighttime emergencies or walks to the PK at night. On one such evening, I had to pee. I was approaching a more modest stage of my life—I would never have considered going outside to squat and pee.

"Mike, hold the lantern for your sister and walk her down to the PK," said Mum.

Mike said something like, "Can't PK take herself?" Being two years older, he really didn't want to babysit me.

Mum opened her mouth to reply to Mike's smart question. She had real gold fillings in her teeth. We always thought it a bit mystical that our mother had a mouth full of gold, unlike the unglamorous silver stuff in our molars. Mike saw the glint of gold and decided it was better to pick up the lantern and lead me down the path.

We stepped over the patio and onto the sandy dirt path. It was too narrow for the two of us to walk side by side, so I followed right behind him. Mike said, "I'm going to scare the snakes up, so they come around and bite you."

"I'm going to tell Mum you're being mean," I responded. I could see his shoulders shrug under his grey khaki shirt. The gesture meant, "Go ahead."

The PK was large and airy. Constructed of *mopani* poles, the walls were never plastered with mud so there was definitely an air of openness. On top of the circular hut was a perfect thatch roof. It had been constructed in layers to create a design of longer and shorter thatch. The hut was about eight feet in diameter, with a packed dirt floor. In the middle was a concrete square "throne," plastered smooth with a skim coat of cement. Crowning that was a black rubbery plastic toilet seat. There was no door — just a rectangular opening.

I always practiced a ritual as I was entering the hut. I would look straight up to make sure there wasn't a *boomslang* (Afrikaans for tree snake) hanging down ready to get me. Next, I would peer over the top of the square throne and look to make sure there wasn't a snake coiled on the back side. Finally, I would look straight at the toilet seat and down into the hole. Just making sure there wasn't one hanging in the PK pit, ready to sink its fangs into my bum.

Mike was in a hurry to get back up the hill. He stood at the entrance of the PK, holding the lantern. "Just go ahead and go in," he said. I complied, skipping my usual ritual. I unzipped my shorts, which fell to my ankles, and sat down on the black plastic toilet seat.

Just then, Mike yelled, "Don't move, there's a cobra five feet from your butt." The cobra, already hooded, was directly behind me and slightly to the right. From my seat on the throne, I could see his shadow from the light of the lamp. The cobra was hovering, ready to strike.

There was no way I was going to stay perfectly still. I lunged forward, throwing myself through the entryway, shorts and *brooks* (panties) around my ankles, and ran straight up the hill, screaming.

MY FAVORITE SNAKE STORIES

Despite being impeded with clothing still dangling around my ankles, I made it to the top of the hill first. As I huffed and puffed to Mum what had just happened, she pulled out our .410 single-shell shotgun. We called it a "snake gun" because it had outperformed itself in being handy and we had killed a lot of snakes with the little weapon. Dad had owned it since his high school years.

She slipped a shell in the shotgun, handed it to me, and said, "Go back down and take care of it." By then, my shorts were snapped and zipped back into place. I grabbed the gun, and Mike and I went back down to the PK. No snake. Where had it gone in such a short time?

We backed out of the PK and Mike had a brilliant idea. He thought if he began to swing the lantern back and forth, he would become an instant snake charmer. When I asked him what he was doing he said, "I read it somewhere."

I stood slightly off the path approximately two or three feet from the hut, dubious that my lantern-swinging brother was going to accomplish what he thought he would, with the shotgun in my right hand, the barrel pointed straight down at the ground.

Suddenly, out of the corner of my right eye, the cobra came up out of the grass. Five feet of him—all excepting the coils on the ground—hurtled straight for my thigh. I didn't have enough time to jump clear of it, but I moved to the left, pointing the barrel of the gun straight away from my leg. Needless to say, I didn't *squeeze* the trigger as I had been taught—I jerked on it as hard as I could.

Boom! The air immediately smelled acrid. Pellets scattered everywhere, kicking up dust and dry grass. I was so close that dirt clogged my nostrils as I looked around.

"Crap, sis, you killed him," said Mike. "Champion shot!"

I had blasted the cobra in two, about a foot below its head.

Then, transitioning from screaming exclamation to quiet nonchalance without skipping a beat, my brother looked at me and said, "Now, let's go to bed."

We hurried back up the hill and opened the door. Mum had heard the gun go off and was waiting there. She reached for the gun to put it back in the closet. "What did you do with the snake?" she asked.

"Ugh, we left it down there, Mum," we said in unison. What else would the nighttime snake hunters do?

"Go back down there and get it, we want to make sure it's dead."

She pulled the gun back out of the closet and handed me another shell. Mike had not extinguished the lantern, so we went running this time down the hill. When we got to the exact spot, the snake wasn't there. We started looking through the grass. Mike stopped swinging the lantern and I saw it—the snake had involuntarily wiggled and flopped a few feet away.

"Pick it up," said Mike.

"No," I said, "I'm the one that shot it. Besides I have to pee."

So, while I went back into the PK to pee, Mike picked up the snake, grabbed the shotgun and lantern, and headed back up the hill.

Brothers! As soon as I got done, I ran after him, telling him I was going to tell Mum that he'd left me down there without a lantern.

"You just bagged a big ass cobra that nearly killed you and you're afraid of the dark?"

My remonstrances that I was only ten years old just made him walk faster. Once again, I double-timed my pace and fell into step right behind him as he guided us back up the hill.

Mum glanced over where we laid the snake. Satisfied that it wasn't going to be slithering through the bush again, she said, "OK, kids, time to go to bed! Remember to say your prayers."

A few weeks later, Mike decided he had to make a nighttime stroll down the path to the PK. It was almost a full moon. He'd just had a bath and was wearing khaki shorts and had slipped his feet into his favorite suede moccasins. He didn't bother to take a torch or a lantern—the beautiful moonlight was almost as bright as the sun.

All of a sudden, we heard him scream. Mike had stepped onto the path and felt a squish. He hadn't needed a light to know that he had stepped directly on a snake. But he didn't know what kind.

By the time Dad got to him with a light, the snake was moving swiftly to a stack of lumber piled up against a tin shed. Even as it was moving, we could see the dark scales and the distinct white band. It was a *rinkhals* (ring-necked spitting cobra).

I felt a sudden rush of adrenalin. The *rinkhals*, although related to the cobra, is not a true cobra. It rears up, flinging its body forward as far as eight feet to spray poison towards its victim. And yes, it aims for the eyes.

The snake slid straight under the bottom layer of lumber and disappeared. Mum handed Mike the shot gun, Dad held the lantern, and I went to get a rake. It seemed like it took hours for me to flip each board away from the wall of the tin shed.

Anxiety was running full tilt through all of us—we depended on each other for survival. Dad reached in with his long arms and with the rake flipped over the very last board. All hell broke loose as the snake shot straight up the wall.

"There it goes, there it goes!" we yelled.

BOOM! Mike killed the snake and it slid down the wall onto the ground. As we looked at where the snake landed, to our horror, we saw that the ground was crawling with baby snakes. The *rinkhals* delivers its young live and we had found her nursery.

It was foolish to start shooting into the ground so Dad started hacking the young snakes with the rake. He yelled to me to get a shovel and help out. We killed as many of the baby snakes as we could before they disappeared in the dark of the night.

When we finished, we looked at Dad. Both his knees were bleeding. Mum pulled him into the light and examined him—his knees were filled with buckshot.

We exploded into punchy bush humor. "Good going, Mikey, you big game hunter," I said. "You mowed Dad down at the knees, all because of a snake."

As before, we returned to the house and went to bed.

Years later, though, Mike got me back. I'd come in from a day of playing tennis and a night of dancing and a little rum and coke at the local police station. The house was very quiet when I climbed into my bed, but my behind never connected with the sheets.

HOTDOGS for HYENAS

I immediately knew what my foot had touched. I went right over the top of my bed, screaming that a snake was in the middle of it. By that time of night, the generator had been turned off to conserve on fuel, so I flipped on my battery-powered bedside lamp.

Mike appeared at my bedroom door and leaned casually against the door frame. Way too calm, I reasoned, and I flipped the covers back. He had killed a snake, cut the head cleanly off, laid it on newspaper, and then placed it on my pretty pink sheets.

Grinning, my brother said, "*Boeremeisie*, it's good to hear you scream," and then turned from the door. "Sleep well."

Several years later, while I was home from college on break, I was on my way out to Nuanetsi to collect the weekly mail and play some tennis, followed by a *braai* (barbeque) and dancing. Our neighbors' ranch of 10,000 acres had nine gates or cattle guards to cross over.

Driving the Land Rover meant I could zip through the cattle guards. During the war years, these slowdowns or pauses were somewhat precarious. If driving the truck, two people had to make the trip—one to open the gates and the other to drive through. Because of terrorist activities, the passenger would jump out of the truck as it slowed down and run for the gate latch. The truck would zip through. The person closing the gate would literally run to close the gate and jump back in the truck.

Nighttime travel was more tenuous because the sound of a vehicle could be heard for miles. I learned with the Land Rover to shift the gears down to second and cross through the cattle guards without ever having to stop. This made for a safer situation.

Once, while I was on my way, my family needed to alert me of potential danger. There was no way to contact me directly, so they took off in the Cessna 206 and spotted me as I drove through one of the cattle guards. As a signal, they dropped brown paper bags of flour in front of me. The message was clear. "Turn around immediately."

But terrorists and airplane flour bombs were not my problem on this particular day. As I headed across the neighbor's ranch on the way to get our mail, I drove around a sandy curve. The road was in good condition so I was able to make the curve at 35 miles an hour. Relaxed, I dangled my arm out the window, soaking up the penetrating sun, when I spotted a mamba just ahead on the driver's side of the road.

Mambas are known to travel via their muscular tails and hurtle towards their targets. Averaging eight feet in length, they present a formidable threat.

I jerked the wheel to the left, careening in the deep sand, and pulled my arm in. Simultaneously, I slid the window back, slamming it shut at the very same instant the mamba struck. I was still holding on to the sliding section of the window when the mamba crashed into the glass. The strike was so close I could see the inside of its black mouth.

In an instant, the ordeal was over. I glanced in the rear-view mirror and saw the snake drop to the ground, every bit alive, and slither across the road. My pulse pounded in my ears.

My family learned to cope with dangerous situations such as these by resorting to comedy. So, when I got home that night, I related the story of the mamba, adding a final punctuation to the tale. "No matter what, the pony express mail must go through."

At times, I recall Africa as serene, quiet, safe, and ideal—but in actuality, the daily threats to my family's existence defy understanding in a civilized society. The image of the mamba's mouth against the window of the Land Rover will forever be etched in my mind.

11
HUNTING

I looked down at the pink frothy drops of blood along the trail. Tiny droplets spewed by the injured zebra left dark telltale evidence on the slab of rough granite outcropping beneath our feet. Lung shot. Missed the head or heart. Mortally wounded, but not yet dead. Our tracker, Tobiya, squatted down to see what direction the injured animal appeared to head.

I hated this. This wasn't what was supposed to happen. I was upset. If I'd known there was such a word as being pissed, I would have been that too. Why was I being made the designated babysitter today?

In the 1960s, safari hunting was high on the list for the elite, including some close friends. My cardiologist was no exception. Dr. James Wood of the Portland, Oregon-based Wood-Starr Heart Team (developed one of the largest heart surgery centers and Teflon heart valve) had hands that were insured for a million dollars and money to buy big game hunting rifles but couldn't sight an animal in the cross-hairs worth a damn. Not even with a precision-fine sighted scope. He had "buck fever," Dad said. Just nervous when he was hunting.

Jim Wood was fit, and he was handsome. His dark hair was starting to grey slightly at the temples. He took care of my heart as a young girl and years later, when I was in college, would invite me to watch him perform open heart surgeries at St. Vincent's Hospital in

Portland, Oregon. He would proudly tell me about the patient and what he was going to do ahead of time.

He was disappointed when I turned down the invitations to move in with his family while attending college, and work summers and vacations for him. To his staff, he was the proverbial instrument-throwing surgeon. To me he was a perfectionist. Once, when I was in college, I saw him personally lift a four-year old patient, the little girl in blonde pig tails, and lay her on the operating table. He looked up at me in the overhead observation gallery. His mask covered his face, but I could see the intense look in his eyes. It was dead serious. He was all about this child. I loved observing the miracles he performed. I could sense the strong odor of pride and determination. He saved many from a certain premature death of heart disease.

As a teenager in Africa, I would visit local villages with Jim, where the women would prepare dishes made from *monga* (a seed type millet used when maize is not available), and a freshly killed chicken dressed in some unknown "spices." The scrawny lice-infested chicken just moments before had been running around the village. The women would grind the *monga* seeds on a carved-out rock or a stand-up mortar with a pestle, then carry the residue to a boiling pot of water to make a grey-colored gritty porridge. On our walk back to the mission, Jim would stop, light a cigarette, and start spitting *monga* seeds that had gotten stuck in his teeth. "Pam, what in the hell was this shit we just ate?" he would ask.

"At least we weren't served black goat," I said.

"Black goat? How did you know?"

"The hair was still on it," I said casually. Today, I wonder how we know whether we're actually eating Black Angus beef.

Jim's prowess in many aspects of American life was fodder for legends. But as far as the big game hunting was concerned, he had met his match. He couldn't hit the broad side of a barn door.

He would clutch; he would seize up. When an impala was killed (normally by my brother) for meat and the buck trussed for dressing, Jim would put on surgical gloves (to protect his assets) and guide me through what he called "blunt dissection." He would hover over my left shoulder — I could smell the faint manly odor of his last Marlboro cigarette mixed with the sweet pungent aroma of his cologne.

In the deep echo of his baritone voice, he would softly whisper, "Just use the tip of the knife. There that's it. Don't go any deeper." He was clearly the master, unflappable, and I was the eager student.

The connecting tissue just below the hide would separate from the meat as I carefully opened a small space. I would make strokes from top to bottom, a few inches at a time. Then he would say, "Now turn your knife around and use the butt of the handle to open the space a bit more."

Surgeons know instinctively how to extract every benefit from their tools. Sharp blade for cutting the tissue, switch ends, and the handle helps efficiently loosen the hide from the flesh in a blunt fashion.

"Easy, easy, don't be in a hurry. Why aren't you wearing gloves by the way? All that stuff gets up under your nails and I don't want to sit across the dinner table from you tonight like that." The banter along with the lessons would continue until we completed our mission to dress out the entire carcass.

I learned to rotate the tip of the blade and the handle like a drum major with his baton. Back and forth, until the hide completely separated from the buck. I can say because of those lessons, I learned not to nick the hide which would have expanded into a quarter size hole once tanned.

I know our trackers thought Jim was crazy and probably went home telling their families about what the fanatical doctor from across the Atlantic Ocean did today. They thought wearing gloves to skin a buck was among the funniest and most bizarre things they'd ever seen. Thankfully, Jim couldn't understand the Shona language. He was oblivious to every word they were saying. They ridiculed him with abandon. I had to bite my tongue. Merging two civilizations, I was the intermediary.

Jim wanted to shoot a zebra and have the hide on his office floor back in Portland. Lest you think for one minute that *our* hunting expeditions were solely for trophies to be mounted, understand that the meat was used to feed the staff at the mission. The other end of the spectrum of hunting was for protection of cattle and human lives. At least once a year we experienced an epidemic of livestock attacks by a leopard. We would set out traps. Our personal game hunting was confined to furnishing meat for the table and maintaining the safety of our herds and livestock.

I think Dad was weary of all Jim's near misses, so he decided he needed to focus his work on the clinic and sent me out with Jim and the tracker. One of the most amazing characteristics of trackers is they can lead you through the bush until you know you are hopelessly lost and bring you right back to the vehicle hours later. We parked and headed out on foot. Tobiya was slightly ahead of us. He slowed to a stop and said, "There." With an outstretched hand, he motioned toward a small herd of zebra — they were not fifty yards ahead. Despite their brilliant black and white markings, zebra appear brilliantly camouflaged in the bush. A few of the herd members sniffed the air, then returned to pulling up savannah grasses.

Jim took the weapon out of the sling around his shoulders. There wasn't even a scrawny tree to steady himself against. He decided to drop to one knee to stabilize his body and raised the rifle to his shoulder. The tracker had already identified which zebra should be selected. The eye line to it was perfect.

Jim fired. The zebra should have dropped with the first shot. Instead it wheeled around, made its distinctive "qua ha" sound and made hooves through the bush. We ran to the spot. Blood was spattered on the ground, and that wasn't good. My brother and I had been taught never to have an attitude of "That's okay — we'll try someplace else." You tracked the animal — you didn't leave it to become the meal for a predator. You didn't maim animals.

So the tracking began. It was hard to pick up blood on the red earth. At first, the zebra was keeping up with the herd. Then it slowed — standing by rocks for a while before moving off. It was there

HUNTING

that I knelt down to discover frothy bright blood and was sickened, knowing that this animal was suffering.

We continued the quest for a couple miles of scrub but finally lost the trail. We never located the zebra or the herd. Our walk back to the Land Rover was interminably long and made all the worse with heavy silence. Jim was visibly shaken.

Not all hunting stories have happy endings, replete with photos of smiling people taken along with their trophy. There is a very real spiritual element to hunting. If we take the welfare of animals into our hands, we have a responsibility of stewardship. I abhor poaching and I am opposed to baiting or tree stands. I hate to attach sport with hunting because hunting was a part of our symbiosis with nature. But I have a huge respect for weapons and the culture of hunting, which can differ from country to country. While I was waiting out the Rhodesian bush war in Europe in the mid '70s, I enrolled in a German hunting course. The protection and selection of game and protocol is unlike anything I had experienced. I was the first American woman to pass the German hunting exam and be licensed to hunt there.

There will always be a special spot in my heart for the recently deceased Dr. James Wood. We had a special bond — our interests in art, German sports cars, symphony, ballet, and the olives from his martinis (My first and last martini was dumped out.) But I never asked him what prompted his passion to hunt. Was it to say he had done it? Was this part of his bucket list?

As I look back, I'm sure there was a certain amount of embarrassment on his part about not bringing in game. Whatever the experience he relished and longed for, it shaped my adolescence. Up until that moment of the zebra hunt, I had a cavalier attitude about death. I was very much immersed in the harshness of the bush and the culture that life was cheap. It surrounded us in Africa. We took it in stride.

But as I swiped my two fingers through the blood left from the lung shot zebra, I didn't know if I ever wanted to take someone out on safari hunt again. As it happens, I never did.

Several years before the hunting incident with Dr. Wood, I had had my own first experience with bringing down a buck. I had used the rifle from the age of six, when my father had taught me to shoot.

Dad had me lie prone on the ground. He set up a target in a cow pasture peppered with sloppy cow poop. The recoil of the .30-.30 was sharp and even though I had the butt firmly against my shoulder, I felt my body move backwards with the force akin to a bumper car. Dad reassured me the recoil I experienced when target practicing was hardly felt when one shot game. (Tell that to a whimpering six-year-old.)

I wasn't terribly excited about repeating this target practice exercise. And to top this off, there was a bull pawing at us under a tree. I saw my dad take his side arm out of the holster, while leading me to safety. I won't claim a great time was had by all. I was being taught survival skills necessary to live in the bush. Dad was doing his best to continue to protect and shelter me but some lessons could not be postponed indefinitely. Although only six years old, I had to learn to handle a firearm.

The *Mau Mau* uprising in Kenya in the early 1950s taught those of us living in isolated areas a lesson. If you wanted to survive, you never let your household help or trackers have access to your weapons. Farmers, missionaries, and families lost their lives during the uprising because of rebels' over-familiarity of family habits and access to weapons. Our household rules were so stringent that our trackers were not even allowed to carry our weapons for us at any time. Never. The Rhodesian government also mandated that every weapon had to be registered.

Each member of my family had at least two weapons registered in his or her name and the local police kept a list. At any time, they could pop in and ask to verify the weapons in the gun safe with the manifest they had in hand.

And we didn't have a little flimsy gun case. It was built into the wall of my parents' bedroom. Constructed of concrete block, there were special recesses for every weapon. On the floor of the gun safe

HUNTING

was another safe that housed cash for payroll and ammunition. It had an extremely heavy steel door that was flush with the wall and a handle that lifted up and locked with a key.

Mum had the door painted the same *mushi* (very nice) seafoam green she painted her bedroom. It softened the reality of our life. I think if she could have made draperies covering the safe door to make it look pretty, she would have done that too.

When the houseboy came in to clean the bedroom, Mum was always present. I'm not sure what she was doing to look busy, but she was vigilant. The room was always impeccable; it only needed daily sweeping and a once a week floor wax.

Our floors were colored black—there was a choice of red, green, or black—with a skim coat of slick concrete. They were polished daily because walking on them scuffed them up, leaving tracks. Every morning our floor looked fresh and the smell of Cobra brand wax wafted through the house, leaving a distinct air of freshness.

It didn't take long to figure out why most other households selected the red or green coating. The bottom of our bare feet had to be scrubbed every night because they too were now black. Even so, our floors always looked great.

Several years had passed since my first target practice session. It was late afternoon, and we were driving past an open almost park-like area, unlike the normal scrub bush. Here, the grass was always green, the trees shady. It beckoned us to stop and have a picnic.

But we never stopped. We were always in a hurry to get home before nightfall. As we slowed to admire this little Eden, we spotted a steenbok. Steenboks are rather small animals with rust-colored coats and large ears, and stand around 24" at the shoulder. The males have straight, spiky black horns. Unlike other bucks that live in herds, the steenbok are generally solitary animals.

I was sitting next to the window of the lorry (Dodge truck). Dad never said a word. His customary signal was to shift the gears down, push in the clutch, take his hand off the gear shift and with the palm of his hand tap the bench seat. I had watched him go through this same routine with my brother for years. Now it was my time. I slowly rolled down the window. The dust trail we created from the drive suddenly swirled inside the truck covering my nose and mouth. I picked the Winchester .30-30 up from its leaning position against the seat. I pulled down the lever action on the little Model 94 and pushed the lever back up. The rifle was cocked. Dad turned off the diesel engine. The vibration stopped, and I could steady the barrel on the extension arms of the truck door mirrors. Still sitting in the seat, I pivoted myself, so I had a straight shot.

The air was so still. No breeze. The buck turned his head. I lined up the open sights. Squinted one eye. Knowing Dad's penchant for not wanting me to dilly dally or lose the night's dinner, I had to be spot on. I pulled the trigger. I felt no recoil. Birds chattered, sending out warning messages. As I lifted my cheek from the gun, the buck was down. "Wow," said my brother, "you did it and it's a head shot. You didn't even mess up the meat!" My first contribution to the family larder. I was only eleven and a girl at that!

I still have the hide from that steenbok — it has a permanent place on the back of my rocking chair. Whenever I move, the hide is the first thing I pack. As the years and moves have rolled by, the hide is starting to look a little shopworn, but it's a constant reminder to me that in Africa, at least, even young children are an integral part of the function of the family unit.

Other hunting stories remain with me, including hunting guinea fowl with the same .30-.30. As I approached the birds, I took careful aim at one. Just as I squeezed the trigger, a guinea fowl on the right side ran left while another on the left darted right. Three in one shot! I shrieked with laughter. Who would believe such a story? The only proof I had was a single shell casing and three guinea fowl.

I enjoyed target practice. We didn't have fancy targets. Just a cardboard box with the front cover of Mum's *Women's Wear* magazine taped to the box. Ammo was expensive because much of it was imported from the U.S. With international sanctions levied by nearly every nation in the world against Rhodesia after our 1965

HUNTING

independence, ammo was considered "very dear." Target practice wasn't a social event at a target range as it's shown today.

When I was fourteen, I was practicing with a Colt .45. After firing, I tilted the barrel up and blew the smoke off. I was Annie Oakley. I was just like a Western cowgirl. I never knew how long my dad's arms were until that day. He grabbed the pistol from me, told me that was a good way to lose my entire head and life and he'd better never see me pull a stunt like that again.

Then there was the hunt I wasn't allowed to go on because I *was* a girl. Dad said if anything happened to me, Mum would never forgive him. They were going after Cape buffalo. Extremely dangerous and deadly, buff are hard to bring down because they have an overlapping ribcage. And incredible stamina. They are often shot with a .375 or .458 and are known to run straight at the hunter, killing him even when they've been shot through the heart.

The buff hunt I wasn't allowed to go on. Dad with Cape buffalo.

HOTDOGS for HYENAS

A neighbor shot one and then leaned his rifle against a tree. His back turned, he never saw the buff resurrect himself. It slammed him against the tree, killing him instantly. The buffalo's massive *boss* (horns that cover the front of the skull) was hung in the local police station. Years later, as our neighbor's widow crossed through the doorway, the boss fell off the wall, barely missing her.

Because of the density of the boss, it is nearly impossible to get a decent head shot. My brother Michael, neighbor Bob Gawler, his brother-in-law Mike Jones, and Dad, all excellent hunters took extreme care that night. The bull Dad shot, through its heart and lungs, stayed on his feet for seven hours before finally expiring. It refused to go down for hours.

My mother had a routine and we dared not mess up her ritual, particularly on Saturday. She prepared all the Sunday school materials, which meant cranking out little bi-fold brochures on an old mimeograph machine for the children to color. She then colored the European featured flannel graph Bible characters with ebony skin tones. After she finished, and she had dinner started, while thawing meat for the next day, she took her bath, washed her hair, set her hair in rollers and wrapped a scarf around her head to hide the rollers.

That particular Saturday, my boyfriend from South Africa was visiting. The son of a Pretoria attorney, Trevor had already served his mandatory military service in South Africa and a tour in Rhodesia as a member of the BSAP (British South Africa Police). He was now working for the Nestle Corporation in Pretoria, South Africa. Trevor was an avid sportsman—he enjoyed rugby, tennis, and hunting. He had a close relationship with my parents and could virtually do no wrong. But that day we tested the limits with Mum.

Trevor and I left the mission around 11 a.m. to play tennis at the Nuanetsi Police Station 40 miles away. Back then, we wore customary tennis whites. My dress even had the frilly panties underneath so when I served the ball and my dress went up, proper etiquette was still being observed. Very proper. Very British.

HUNTING

We had a great time, followed by a swim and a *braai*. We were heading home when we braked for a herd of impala. Trevor was beside himself. To him, bringing home an impala was the perfect ending of a perfect day.

But it was late Saturday afternoon. Mum was the butcher of meat. She was particular. No one could cut a filet like she could. She wouldn't let us even help. Bringing in an impala was really going to screw up her routine. But we *did* need the meat and Trevor was such a good shot. With a mischievous smile, we bounded out of the Land Rover. With one shot, we headed through the brush in our spanky white duds, including white *tackies* (tennis shoes). Trevor dragged the impala to the Landy and loaded her through the back door. We soon pulled into the driveway next to the house and Mum was outside watering some plants.

"Well there's no time like the present to tell her," I said.

True to form, Mum was close to retiring for the evening—her hair in the customary scarf and her face smelling of Ponds cold cream. She eyed us as we opened the back door of the Land Rover.

"Mum, come look at what we brought you," I said in my most chipper voice. She started walking towards us.

"Where is Dad?" I thought. He would have been saving our butts right now. He was our ally, defending our contribution or at least softening the blow.

Mum never raised her voice at us. To this day, I have never heard her yell. But that Saturday, she was mad. She pulled the scarf down around her ears.

Lamely, we offered to take over the butcher job. She looked at us standing so spiffy in our tennis togs with not a dirt mark or a drop of blood anywhere on our clothes.

"You know it's Saturday, don't you?" she said.

"Yes, Mum," I said. If I had thought a royal curtsy would have helped at that moment, I would have given her that.

She turned and walked up to the shop where the impala would be trussed and quartered. About that time, Dad came walking out of his office. He raised his eyebrows upon seeing the "gift" we had brought home. He shook his head, gave us a wink, turned around and walked back in the office. He was going to make this our *ndaba* (discussion).

There weren't a whole lot of pleasantries exchanged during dinner that night and we apologized profusely to no avail.

The next afternoon we were down on the banks of the Nuanetsi. We went to see if we could spot the elusive 12-foot croc that kept our drinking water clean. The African children were afraid to play in the deep-water hole because the croc was — well he was a croc — cantankerous and aggressive. He was known to grab a goat and drag it under. Crocs were royal game (protected). You had to have a permit to hunt one and, if you shot one without a permit, you'd better have a pretty good reason.

Trevor and I had my Doberman with us. Dobie jumped from rock to rock, all in for whatever excitement we could stir up. I had a leather-braided leash with me just in case she wandered too close to the water. We walked the mile or so down to the river, Dobie looping around periodically making sure we were keeping up with her. It had rained the night before, so we could see croc tracks. We followed them looking behind us every so often. Inside a little inlet we found eggs. The croc we'd called "he" for years, was a mama!

We knew she had to be close. I had a long stick with me and rolled one of the eggs closer. I'd never seen croc eggs. We climbed across huge rocks and crossed the river to find a spot to croc watch.

"Hand me the camera, please," said Trevor. "I want to take some photos of you near the river." I sat down and slipped off my sandals as he walked a few feet away.

Croc watching on the Nuanetsi (Mwenezi)

HUNTING

The dog was still off her leash. Just as he pushed the shutter, we heard a huge smacking sound of the croc's tail. She was coming over the rock where I was sitting. Straight at me. I grabbed the Colt .45 that I had placed to my right, the leash to the left. Trevor grabbed the dog with one hand and me with the other. "*Meisie,*" he said, "run like bloody hell!"

We pelted up the rock and ran parallel to the river, scrambling across tumbled boulders. When we got to safety on the other side of the river, I looked down at my feet. "I left my sandals back on the rock," I said.

Trevor, ever the gentleman offered to go back, but I wouldn't let him. "It's better to cut my losses with the footwear than go back." I didn't want him to anyway. I was jumpy with every sound I heard.

Once we got back to the house, we cleaned up and changed for dinner. I set the table, carefully laying all the silver for several courses with dessert fork and spoon at the top of the plates, drinking goblets perfectly set to the upper right, and folded the serviettes (napkins).

My mind wasn't on what I was doing. I was thinking of the overlapping teeth and the long toenails of the croc coming straight at me.

During dinner, Dad said, "I hope the two of you had a much less eventful day than yesterday." Trevor was sitting directly across the table from me. We didn't even have to kick each other under the table. But sooner or later, I knew the question of my missing sandals would come up, so we had to come clean. I tried to lighten the potential seriousness of the situation. "We coulda brought you a croc handbag," I said to Mum. And then, before I got into more trouble with my mother, Trevor and I slipped out the door to pack up the little orange Karmann Ghia for his 400-mile trip back to South Africa.

12
EDUCATION

It may sound odd that parents who were eking out an existence in the African bush, sometimes traumatically on a daily basis, would insist their daughter study the classics and develop skills of recitation, but my parents were fully engaged in that arena. They expected my brother and me to eventually, and seamlessly, step in to a university to continue our education. *Caedmon's Hymn* composed between 658 and 680 A.D., *Beowulf,* The *Iliad and the Odyssey*, Henry Wadsworth Longfellow's *Wreck of the Hesperus*, Robert Frost's *The Road Not Taken* were a small but significant part of my daily regimen of studies.

I vividly recall keeping my horse up in her *kraal* so I would have a sympathetic audience as I memorized the *Wreck of the Hesperus*. Unlike an American horse corral, with the boards placed in a horizontal position with enough space to climb in between the boards or a smooth top board to sit on, the African cattle-type *kraal* poles are placed tightly together vertically. I would find a way to climb up the nearly six-foot poles and balance myself on the sharp narrow pole tops. From there I would glance down at my book, memorize a few lines and recite them to my indifferent audience of one.

She was clearly unimpressed with my hand gestures and decisive voice inflections as I memorized my least favorite assignment for the morning (which I believe often stretched into days). I was positive that I would never have any purpose for this work anytime in my life and my horse seemed to concur as she impatiently pawed at the gate begging me to cease and desist so she could escape her quarters and graze.

My home schooling had its drawbacks, but there is nothing to compare to treasured memories of my dad singing songs or reciting poetry to me. Any American songs I learned I owe to him. *Red River Cowboy* would mean an open invitation to come sit by his side.

Some of his favorite songs were those he sang to my mother while courting her in the 1940s. I don't recall ever asking him to read me a story or poetry — he just did. It would typically be after dinner near sunset.

He memorized everything. Edgar Allen Poe's *Annabel Lee*, Alfred Noyes's *The Highwayman*, and then there was Vachel Lindsey's rendition of *The Congo*. I knew the lines by heart but would squeal and laugh at the exaggerated emotion Dad would pour into this poem. Over a half a century later, I can remember every pause, every emphasis, as he would orate with the brilliant fiery orb of an African sunset behind him:

FAT black bucks in a wine-barrel room,
Barrel-house kings, with feet unstable,
Sagged and reeled and pounded on the table,

And then with a deep rolling base, Dad would continue:

Pounded on the table,
Beat an empty barrel with the handle of a broom,
Hard as they were able,
Boom, boom, BOOM,
With a silk umbrella and the handle of a broom,
Boomlay, boomlay, boomlay, BOOM.
THEN I had religion, THEN I had a vision.
I could not turn from their revel in derision.

EDUCATION

And with nearly a chant, Dad would say:

THEN I SAW THE CONGO, CREEPING THROUGH THE BLACK,
CUTTING THROUGH THE FOREST WITH A GOLDEN TRACK.

Then along that riverbank
A thousand miles
Tattooed cannibals danced in files;
Then I heard the boom of the blood-lust song
And a thigh-bone beating on a tin-pan gong.

And then the booming climax would begin...

And "BLOOD" screamed the whistles and the fifes of the warriors,
"BLOOD" screamed the skull-faced, lean witch-doctors,
"Whirl ye the deadly voo-doo rattle,
Harry the uplands,
Steal all the cattle,
Rattle-rattle, rattle-rattle,
Bing!
Boomlay, boomlay, boomlay, BOOM,"
A roaring, epic, rag-time tune

Dad's voice would soften as if he was whispering to a baby he was holding in his arms.

From the mouth of the Congo
To the Mountains of the Moon.
Death is an Elephant,
Torch-eyed and horrible,

Now Dad would go at it in full force as if he was standing alone on a battlefield. White flecks of saliva would gather at the corners of his mouth:

Foam-flanked and terrible.
BOOM, steal the pygmies,
BOOM, kill the Arabs,
BOOM, kill the white men,

Dad would pause, exhale and speak as if he was trying to be heard over an imaginary windstorm.

HOO, HOO, HOO.
Listen to the yell of Leopold's ghost
Burning in Hell for his hand-maimed host.
Hear how the demons chuckle and yell
Cutting his hands off, down in Hell.
Listen to the creepy proclamation,
Blown through the lairs of the forest-nation,
Blown past the white-ants' hill of clay,
Blown past the marsh where the butterflies play: —
"Be careful what you do,
Or Mumbo-Jumbo, God of the Congo,

And finally, my father's voice would grow softer until he whispered the last line:

And all of the other
Gods of the Congo,
Mumbo-Jumbo will hoo-doo you,
Mumbo-Jumbo will hoo-doo you,
Mumbo-Jumbo will hoo-doo you." (Lindsay, 1914)

Although we began our African journey primitively, colonial Africa was not always a place of desolation, but a place of splendid culture. We used 12-piece cutlery (the fish fork and fish knife were distinctly different than the rest of the silverware) at meals, tea was

EDUCATION

served twice a day—half past nine in the morning and again at four p.m. We would gather in chairs on the veranda.

While having a cup of tea may seem mundane to today's consumers—tea bag in a cup of water, heat in microwave—our teatime was precious. It was time spent rejuvenating our souls, bringing us together to discuss politics, local news, authors, books, projects and giving us all a sense of well-being. It was ceremony.

The tea tray would be brought out with the tea pot covered in a floral pink tea cozy, raw sugar and fresh milk in china receptacles, complete with the traditional net covering to keep the flies out.

Mum, an excellent baker always had something fresh to serve. If we had recently returned from town, apple turnovers from a bakery in Bulawayo were served as a treat. A holiday tea treat was when Mum made *koeksisters* (pronounced "cook sisters"). She would braid dough, deep fry these delicacies, and drizzle them in a sugary syrup. That 15- to 20-minute break in our arduous routine was heaven.

While it was a time to gather for us, it was also a time to check our dogs over for encounters with blood-sucking ticks and worms. Flies would deposit eggs in the skin of our dogs, which would develop into maggots. The small boils created from the infestations were easily recognizable on the dog's shiny coats. While lifting a cup of tea in one hand, we would pop grub-size worms out with a safety pin with the other hand.

Once a week I played tennis doubles with friends, where everyone engaged in world politics over a drink and *braai* (cookout) afterwards. We were much more adept and engaged in what was happening throughout the world than I later found Americans to be outside of their borders.

During one of these outings, I stopped at a nearby ranch to have tea with an ailing family friend. Nearing the end of her life, she graciously offered me a cup of tea. I sat on the edge of her bed, catching up on her family news. Finally, she took both of my hands in hers and said, "Pamela dear, don't ever marry someone who will not return you to Africa." We never dreamed at that moment that her children—and I—would not have the luxury of growing old in the country we held so dear to our hearts.

When we were in Bulawayo for monthly supply shopping, we attended the ballet, theater, and wonderful parties. However, at home in the bush, when my studies were done for the day, I had the freedom of taking off and exploring a cave—more like an alcove, five miles from our home.

Once there, I would climb over a quarter-acre slab of rough granite and, close to the opening, absorb the historical significance of the Bushmen or San paintings on the wall. Back then we never referred to these paintings as the works of the San, only Bushmen. The ochre paint was still brilliant even though clearly exposed to the natural sunlight for 5,000 years.

The local Shona treated these treasures cavalierly. They would shrug and say, "*Handizivi* (I don't know), they were from ancient peoples."

There were lots of similar paintings around the area. Where had these people come from? They were nomadic people, excellent hunters. And the game, painted in various forms of movement, had apparently once been plentiful in this small region. But no more.

In any case, this cave on the Maranda Tribal Trust was a favorite haunt of mine. I never fully appreciated how privileged I was to have this art gallery, this piece of history, all to myself. Could anything be more ideal? Will I ever be able to find this special spot if I return? Has any other European savored this sight?

The Bushmen, the San, were a part of my education. The art they left us is tangible. Just as I was receiving a European classics education of poetry and the arts, I was receiving an African arts classics education. In my early life, they held equal value. There was no tip of the scales as to which was more important—however, in my twilight years, I treasure my exposure to ancient man in Africa the most. I was raised in what is now the hotbed of research on these ancient peoples.

It's not what we know, it's what we *understand*. Excitingly, we're just scratching at the surface of that. Today, there are perhaps 2,000

EDUCATION

San left in Zimbabwe with only a handful of elders remaining that speak the nearly-extinct language. Most of them are over the age of 60. It's time to not just know about these people, but to understand the legacy they left us. Instead of acknowledging that the San language (Twswari) is nearly extinct we need to ensure that it survives.

Do not think for one minute that my home-schooling was haphazard as I have observed in some programs in America. During my primary school years, The Calvert School from Baltimore, Maryland, was the correspondence institution in which I was enrolled.

It was stringent with a tough curriculum and detailed daily lesson plans and it never deviated. There were no short cuts or sliding by. At no time did my parents hear, "I don't want to do that today."

Morning lessons started immediately after breakfast and seven to nine subjects were covered throughout a full day of study ending around 2 p.m. Latin was introduced in the seventh grade as well as options for extra credit courses. If we traveled, the books and syllabi went with me. Like the European system of education, I attended school year-round with mini-breaks at specific times of the year.

Outside of the normal standard curriculum, I was offered optional courses. I latched onto one in particular: photography. Dad had the latest in 35 mm cameras as well as a Graflex Super Speed Graphic 4x5 press camera.

I loved shooting black and whites. What was even better was developing my own film, much to my mother's horror. She tolerated this hobby of my dad's. Before leaving for Africa, she "allowed" him to develop film in the back of a walk-in closet. (The enlarger, tables, red lights, and trays mysteriously made their way to Africa.)

Now Dad had a comrade in developing — me. He was an excellent instructor, except for one small issue. He forgot to tell me not to wipe my hands-on Mum's bathroom towels. Imagine the outburst after a successful night of developing great photos — when my Mum found reddish stains on her freshly laundered white bathroom towels. If we had owned a doghouse, she would have banished us there indefinitely. After that, when she thought we might spend a night developing, she would rush in and remove any and all things terrycloth, replacing them with dispensable rags.

My high school years were especially tough. The choice was boarding school or correspondence through the University of Nebraska. I opted for boarding school, but my parents overruled, insisting on studies through the university. My mother couldn't bear the thought of having me so far away with visits few and far between. My parents won. I was deeply disappointed. I wanted and needed daily interaction with other students. I yearned for peer socialization.

The school year was divided between semesters and all of my papers were mailed to the university, graded by professors and returned to me in Africa. And still, while traveling, my books went with me. While visiting Agra, India, my parents secured the services of a university professor to sit on the lawn of the Taj Mahal for a one-on-one lecture. The world was my classroom. A positive outcome was my sense of self-discipline towards studying. Consequently, I developed independence in my approach to other interests I would tackle.

Most of my friends were Afrikaans-speaking who attended boarding school in South Africa. In my third year of high school, I lobbied to be sent to school in Pietersburg. Dad employed his art of persuasion. "If I build you a swimming pool, will you stay?"

It worked. While he was placing the handmade blue mosaic tiles around the pool, I would sit on the edge with my heavy-duty modern problems book pumping him with questions. The pool was great—22 by 44 feet, terraced lawn, right outside my bedroom window. Dad even built a small foot pool on either end so we wouldn't have sand or dirt on our feet when we got in the pool.

Then came my senior year. Sadly, my parents were not so intensely involved in my education during the final two years. They relied heavily on my self-discipline to get things done. I hammered out my papers on my favorite grey and pink standard typewriter. I plowed through algebra/trig, chemistry, physics, and German. In the afternoon, I would walk over to the lab at the mission clinic and do gram stains. Often, I would hop up on the concrete counter in the

EDUCATION

lab and with the sun streaming through the window, open a textbook while cranking the centrifuge with my free right hand.

But my interests were shifting. My boyfriend, Trevor, whom I spoke of before, became an increasingly important part of my life. We met when he was investigating the vehicular death of an African bicyclist by a fellow missionary daughter. Vehicular murder charges were being filed and Dad was trying to protect the girl, who was my age. Dad argued that the charges were extreme and would have a lifelong devastating effect on this less than confident young woman.

I was called in to testify on her behalf. She was not present nor were her parents (her father was the mechanic who left the cotter pins in our plane and later sided with Central Africa Mission against my parents). My testimony helped change the mind of the principal investigator and the charges were dismissed. After that, Trevor began to visit our home socially.

The push continued for me to attend school in South Africa. His parents assured my parents they would take good care of me. I made early application to University of Witwatersrand in Johannesburg and the University of South Africa in Pretoria. But first, I needed to transfer to a South African high school. I spent all my spare time in South Africa getting flight time in a Cessna 150 Aerobat, so it all sounded like a logical move to me.

Me in tennis whites and sun hat. Even in the bush we had proper decorum. After a Saturday game of tennis there was time for putt-putt golf, dinner, and dancing.

But my parents said no — they wanted me to attend an American university. For years, I struggled with their decision. I decided early in my life, that despite the superb academic environment I experienced with my parents, I would never home-school my own children under any circumstances.

13
LESSONS IN RESILIENCE

My love for horses predates my memory. At the tender age of two, I was already riding a pony named Victory at my grandparents' farm in Oregon. A photo with curled-up corners reveals a little girl with blond curls, short little legs wrapped tightly to the pony's side, and tiny hands neck reining with a cotton rope tied off as a halter. My dad stands close by Victory's head, looking quite handsome in gaberdine slacks and a white T-shirt, ready to grab me in case of an emergency.

Mum was nowhere in sight. She harbored a deep disdain for horses. She grew up on a farm—horses weren't for pleasure riding, they were working draft horses. Dad bought her a horse when they were first married. He never warned her about her new equine gift—he rode the mare home. Every time Mum would put a foot in the stirrup, the horse would turn and bite her in the bum.

Dad was pretty much in the doghouse and the mare was dispatched to a new home. After that Mum never found the need to warm towards horses. Dad, however, who had grown up in Colorado, instilled in me his love for horses. And his father before him had been an excellent judge of horses and mules.

I had begged for a horse of my own for years. Horses were difficult to maintain in the harsh bush country. Horse sickness (a virus spread by infected midges/gnats) was prevalent. Bont ticks, with their hard, crusty shells, transmitted a virus that maimed animals, and nocturnal animals such as leopards and hyenas were attracted to domesticated horses as easy evening meals.

But my parents finally caved to my continued pleas for horse ownership. It's probably more accurate to say that *Mum* caved. Dad was just waiting for me to be old enough to convince Mum of my responsible nature.

The British South Africa police station at Nuanetsi, 40 miles away from our home, had a black filly they were willing to sell us and it was love at first sight. She had a kind eye and was smallish at about 14.2 hands — perfect for a first horse. Then, days before I was to take delivery of her, she blew snot profusely through her nose, fell over, and died. Horse sickness had struck her. Sturdy horses were hard to come by — and my initial aspirations were squelched.

At the age of 12, I resurrected my quest for a horse. The cattle auction at Rutanga was 50 miles away. Occasionally, a few horses would come up from South Africa and would be thrown into the mix at the auction. I grew up in an Afrikaans-speaking district, so most of the farmers coming to auction spoke Afrikaans.

Dad and I arrived at Rutanga for the auction and everyone wanted to know what it was we were looking for. Yes, a couple of horses had come in, we were told. I wanted to go straight to the holding pen. "No, let's go up on this little rise, sit down with some potato crisps and coke and watch the horses," he said. "You can learn a lot by just watching body language."

I eyed two I liked — a red and white spotted horse and a sorrel. Dad wasn't interested in the spotted horse. "A little too rangy," he said. "Looks like he won't be an easy keeper." So, we watched the sorrel. He asked the auctioneer how old the horse was and the reply was 12 years. Perfect for a young girl.

I registered with the auctioneer to bid and was given a small white piece of cardboard, glued to a stick. "That's your number," said Dad. "Be careful when you raise it. You might buy something you didn't intend to." All the Afrikaans-speaking farmers around collectively

LESSONS IN RESILIENCE

laughed. They joked they'd have me bidding on a prize bull instead of a horse. When all was said and done, I bought the sorrel horse for the equivalent of $12.

But wait, how was the new addition to our family going to get home? We didn't own a horse trailer. All she had on her was an eland hide rope slipped over her neck with a five-foot lead—kind of a *sjam bok* (a stout leather whip).

One of our workers, Tobiya, jumped at the chance of walking the little mare, which I had immediately named "Bonanza," home. (I had heard there was a TV show by that name in America. Only thing I didn't know is that Americans pronounced it differently than we did in Africa. She was Bo-Non-za to us.) Tobiya led her through all the back trails, which ended up being about 25 miles. The next day he proudly walked her up the drive, still holding on to the eland hide rope.

Then, Dad got his first really good look at the mare. After looking at her teeth he said, "Twelve years old, my foot. She's only two years!" He turned to me and my brother and said, "There's two ways of breaking a horse. You can put a blanket on her, then lean on her, then gradually add another blanket for more weight. Do it slow and in about a week she will trust you. Then you can throw a leg over."

"What's the other choice, Daddy?" I asked. "You can swing up on her and ride it out."

Mum was nowhere in sight so I said, "Let me ride her out." Within seconds, I was up on her back…and within seconds, I was on the ground with a mouthful of sand and a bloodied nose.

Bonanza and I had a love/hate relationship. It was my responsibility to put her up at night and that was when the fun would start. She would take off running any time she thought confinement was pending.

We tried hobbling her (roping back legs so she couldn't run), so she'd stay close to the house. That didn't work. She managed to break free and would take off bucking and running with half a hobble dangling from a back leg. Dad finally took a spare VW Kombi tire, attached a chain to it, and then snapped the other end of the chain to her halter. She would still run with it, but this apparatus slowed her down so she was catchable.

Then she discovered how to get the tire up on its edge. This crazy mare would run away with the tire upright. She was skilled at weaving through trees. She reminded me of a motorcycle with a sidecar—the tire being her equine version.

One day, when I was in high school, I decided to spoil her with freedom from her ball and chain for the day. She  had one friend, a big old white egret, that would ride on her withers, picking whatever delicacy he could find in Bonanza's mane. I looked out at them a time or two and commented how peaceful she was with her companion, who looked regal in his white feathers pooping white bird doo-doo on her back.

At dusk, I went to catch her to take her to her *kraal*. She wasn't having it and took off running down the airstrip at a full gallop. After dinner, Dad said, "Pamela you're not coming to bed tonight until your horse is put up."

A visiting college student who had grown up with horses was staying with us. "I'll help you," she said. No sweet feed, peanut butter sandwiches, carrots or bucket of fresh water would tempt my cantankerous mare. We sat cross-legged on a runway marker. Hour after hour ticked by. The college student showed me how to play a card game and then another and then another. We didn't need torches (flashlights); the moon was bright enough to see the cards. (Pretty risqué for me. My parents didn't approve of card games.)

LESSONS IN RESILIENCE

Occasionally, we'd attempt to entice Bonanza with a treat. Finally, at 1 a.m., she was tired. She walked up to where we were sitting, dropped her head, and let me tie her lead on. When I walked in the house, Dad looked at me. "Is she up for the night?" he asked.

I said, "Yes, and when I have children, they will never have an Arabian and they will never have a mare. Only geldings." The first part of the statement I held true to, the other not so. I later owned a lot of brood mares.

In June 1967, when I was 14 years old, our family was readying to travel abroad for several months and Bonanza's disposition became my responsibility. She could not stay at the mission. Now, you have to remember my dad was an advocate for bareback riding. "If you come off your horse, you'd better know how to get back on," I can hear him saying. Shoot, I'd been tossed off this mare so many times, landing in thorn bushes (and having the nasty thorns break off under my skin), that I could hop back up before my feet would hit the ground. We decided that Bonanza would take up residence with our wonderful and accommodating neighbors, Bob and Denise Gawler.

The obvious barrier was the 25 miles of uninhabited bush separating us. I had absolutely no idea how long it would take me to ride through the bush but I woke up full of excitement before the sun rose. I dressed in a pair of jeans and a red, white, and black flannel hand-me-down shirt from my brother. I had forgotten to bring my favorite pair of Bata brand bush baby shoes (a girl's version of *vellies*) in from the kitchen *stoep* (terraced steps) the night before.

Out of habit, I grabbed both sides of the dark brown suede shoes and clunked the heels down on the top step. No scorpions fell out. I slipped my bare feet in and tied the matching brown cloth laces tight.

God, the air felt so good. It was June, winter in southern Africa. I shivered when the temp got down below 69 degrees. Mum, who already had a fire in the fireplace before I got up, handed me a cup of coffee with boiled milk, *"Baie lekker"* (delicious), and I hugged her.

By this time, Mum had grudgingly come to tolerate my horse, who would amble up the sidewalk to the kitchen door and nicker softly. Mum would call out to me, "Your horse is here for her sandwich." She had come to get her daily treat of a peanut butter and jelly sandwich.

"Ja, Mums, you have a soft spot for Bonanza," I thought. And with coffee in hand, I headed for the horse *kraal*. I whistled to Bonanza and she was waiting for me at her gate. With the eland hide lead slipped snuggly around her neck, I led her back up to the sidewalk outside the kitchen door. Mum handed me a tin of Liebig grapefruit, a tin opener, and a canteen filled with water. Dad handed me his treasured Colt .45 and holster. We managed to tie all four items on my belt and slipped it around my waist over the top of my shirt.

I placed both hands close to Bonanza's withers and jumped straight up from the ground but I was so loaded down, I couldn't swing my leg over and slid back down.

I looked at Dad. "This doesn't look so good. I have to be able to get up and over." He bent down and gave me a leg up and I landed firmly in the middle of her back. I neck-reined my little mare to the left and headed away from the house.

My head was eye level with the poinsettia hedge my mother had planted along the driveway. The brilliant red blossoms at the tops of the hedge balanced themselves on skinny stalks. I had no idea where she had gotten these plants, but she could magically grow anything, even if it looked like it could never be revived.

Dobie, my black and tan Doberman, started to follow me. "*Wena hamba* (you go)," I said to her. With obvious disappointment, she walked slowly back to Mum and sat down. I could see she wasn't sitting all the way down on her butt—she was ready to spring into action, positive that at any minute, I'd change my mind and call, *Buya lapa* (come here), and we'd be off on an adventure.

But I didn't. When I got to the end of the drive, I turned and gave the folks a wave and then kicked Bonanza into a little trot. We jogged down around the road to the end of the airstrip. I hopped off at the gate, led Bonanza through it, and secured the latch.

LESSONS IN RESILIENCE

With an extra push of energy, I jumped up on her back. Thank goodness, I knew of only one other place I'd have to dismount before I got to Gawler's house.

I could see the smoke from the fires at the clinic's in-patient huts curling through the scant *mopani* trees. People were already heading in for treatment. "*Mangwanani, Mamuka sei?* (Good morning. Did you get up?)," I said to a mother, who had a bundle of firewood on her head, a baby on her back, and another one at her skirt. "*Tamuka wo, Mamuka sei?* (I got up. Did you get up?)," she asked.

I smiled. "*Tamuka wo.*"

With our customary greeting over, I made my way away from the mission and towards the African store two miles away. I could see the flies buzzing around the 55-gallon drum filled with home-brew *doro* on the back side of the store. How many skulls had we stitched up after our locals had overindulged at this well of wretched smelling alcohol? I nudged Bonanza on.

In another three miles, we reached the dry riverbed of the Dine River. We had laid cut poles across the riverbed to keep from getting stuck. The weekly bus that drove through the Tribal Trust would roar through the riverbed tearing the poles up end over end and never stopping to put them back in place. During the rainy season, the bus would do a repeat performance, get stuck and have to unload all its passengers. The driver would send someone to the mission five miles away and we'd have to winch them out while a group of men would push from behind getting splattered with mud.

Dine River during the rainy season. Bonanza and I made our way across here on our trek.

We also inner-tubed down the Dine during the rainy season, usually around Christmas. During this season, the fast-flowing water was safe from infectious bilharzia. My brother and I would hop on at the crossing, float for five miles, and jump off, tubes in hand, just before getting sucked into the confluence of the turbulent Nuanetsi River. With boulders the size of cars, we would have easily lost our lives should we have ever reached the "point of no return." With clothes, hair and skin saturated with mud, we were nearly unrecognizable except for our grins, as we headed back to the mission, ready to do it all over again.

I moved Bonanza to the right so she wouldn't have to straddle the poles. The riverbank on the other side was not as steep—just a few washouts. Now, Bonanza was curious. Her ears were riveted straight forward.

Another mile, and we veered off to the right and headed on a tire track road, weaving through trees. This was a cutoff to the ranch. When I got to our adjoining fence, I looked for the gatekeeper. Bob had recently moved the gatekeeper to watch that no one slipped through the gate to graze "extra" cattle on his section. He had put the gate in just for us, otherwise it would have been at least an extra 100 miles to get to his homestead.

The gate was kept locked most of the time, but Bob had told the gatekeeper I'd be coming through. I dismounted and led her through the 12-foot gate. I climbed up the top strand of fencing and slid over onto Bonanza. This would be the last time I'd have to dismount and remount until we got to Leopard Rock, five miles from the Gawlers' home.

The gatekeeper called out to me as he sleepily crawled out of his hut. I waved back. I didn't have time to chat—I needed to keep going. This was the last time I saw another human being for the rest of the trip, but bush telegraph reached Bob hours before I arrived at his place that I was well on my way.

The sky was brilliant blue, not a cloud in sight. I half expected to hear Dad flying overhead to check on me, but it was eerily quiet except for a few Go-Away birds.

We rode through a herd of zebra and wildebeest. They sniffed

LESSONS IN RESILIENCE

at us and then lowered their heads and continued grazing. I patted Bonanza on the neck and then eased my feet forward, massaging her neck with the sides of my shoes.

I looked up at the sky. The sun was straight up. Noon. We headed down the backside of the Mulengani dam. This was a major water source Bob had built a few years before. The backside of the dam was rocky, and I let Bonanza pick her own way through. We were 12 miles from home, almost halfway to the Gawlers' house.

Suddenly, Bonanza squealed and snorted, producing guttural sounds from her throat I'd never heard before. My legs, which I had perched on her neck, suddenly fell to her side and she snorted again.

A herd of baboons ran screeching and screaming in front of us. Mothers with babies on their backs. Males with teeth exposed, red backsides flashing, were in front of and behind us. Baboons were tumbling out of the small *kopje* to our left and Bonanza was becoming increasingly hard to handle. No words of "whoa" or "easy" were making her calm. Dust was rolling up to our nostrils. She began to spin and buck.

Within seconds I realized what was happening. A huge leopard leapt out right in front of us, nearly brushing Bonanza's chest. I could count every rosette on its muscular body. Its bared yellowy fangs were within a few feet of my hands. The sounds my horse was making began to pound in my ears. She reared up and I held on to both reins, tucking my legs tighter against her sides.

Bonanza squealed horribly, came up one more time, broke a rein, and off I went. Skidding backwards, I found my back against a fallen tree, my mouth full of sand, and my left hand gripping the broken left rein. My long hair was filled with grit. I laid there for a second stunned at what had just happened and raised up to see Bonanza tearing off through the bush. The lone flailing rein slapped her in the flank and she was gone.

Liebigs Ranch was a million and a quarter acres and the section we were in was 233,000 acres. She could be anywhere. Then I spotted the leopard. I slid my hand over the handle of the .45 and pulled it out. My thumb began to pull back the hammer, but I stopped. The leopard had settled for a not-so-swift baboon and was carrying it back to her home in the rocks. Ignoring me completely, the leopard focused on getting her lunch to her ledge.

I steadied my breathing. She would be occupied for the rest of the day. I was out of danger for the moment, but I knew my horse and I would be in a precarious situation once the sun set in another six hours. I sat down in the dirt, pulled out the tin opener and opened the can of grapefruit. I drank all the juice and then buried the tin close to where I had landed.

"Well I'd better start walking. I'm 12 miles from nowhere," I said to myself. Then, just as I stood up, I saw Bonanza coming toward me.

"Come here, *meisie*," I said. White lather was dripping from her neck, chest and between her legs. She was looking up at the *kopje* where hell had just broken loose.

The remnant of the rein was still attached to the set screw on her bridle. I looked at the other part in my hand and decided I could tie the two pieces of leather together. I laid my forehead against her neck, breathing in the smell of horse sweat and leather as I knotted the two parts of the rein together. I slipped the reins over her neck, jumped up on her back, and we quietly moved away from the leopard's lair.

Bonanza was still lathered from fear, her chest still heaving, but for once, she did not act up. It was not until we had gone another mile that I spoke out loud. "Thanks girl," I said, "we're going to be all right."

We quietly moved on to the last 12 miles. I didn't sing to her to ease her flightiness like I often had. I wanted to get to the final gate at Leopard Rock (named because a leopard had taken up residence years before and could be seen lying on the flat ledge over the top of the road). When we reached it, I slipped off her back and led her through the gate.

Bob and Denise could see Leopard Rock from their front yard. I reached the bottom of their *kopje*—their home and veranda were on the top—and looked straight up.

LESSONS IN RESILIENCE

Bob had told Philemon, one of his workers, to meet me and get Bonanza to a stall and water her. When Philemon reached me, I shook my head no. I would finish riding her to where she needed to go.

I passed the African store with its white-washed walls and the little square black and white sign: "Section 8, G.D. Gawler." We'd made it.

Bob in his khaki shorts, matching shirt, knee socks and boots grinned at me. "Jolly good show, Pam. Jolly good show." Denise was smiling, barefoot in a fresh frock, cigarette in one hand. She handed me a Rose's Lime Juice and water.

"We were starting to get worried about you," she said. It was 6 p.m. Twelve hours to cover 25 miles.

Once Bonanza was settled in, we all headed to the house. Denise had a hot bath drawn for me and a favorite dinner of roast beef, rice, and peas. I told the story of our adventure with the leopard. Bob knew the location of every leopard on his farm, but this one was new to him. Since his cattle were targets for leopards, he was instantly concerned. If they went on a killing spree, he generally set out traps.

The next morning, my parents drove over to pick me up. I was already down at the horse *kraal* with a cup of coffee checking on Bonanza. Satisfied she was in a secure place, my responsibility of taking care of her was done. I could now fly to East Africa, India and Asia. At the young age of 14, I had learned a lifetime of lessons in resilience, lessons in overcoming challenges thrown in my way.

14
THE POWER OF NGANGA

I watched as my parents continually wove the tapestry of African culture with Western medicine. One of the commitments my family made was to build schools, recruit teachers, and educate the people of Maranda Tribal Trust Land. We started with one classroom. Dad formulated molds for cement and hired laborers, and every day they would crank out cement bricks.

In the past, bricks were made from dirt from the white ant (termite) hills, mixed into mud, and then stacked together to make a kiln. The exterior was covered in mud and a fire built in a hollowed-out center of the brick pile. Dad had already built one school using this method, but decided for longevity, cement brick and block was the most financially advantageous way to build the new structures.

The school we built on this mission site was made entirely of cement bricks, plastered on the outside and painted white. Galvanized tin roofs were placed over rafters imported from Canada.

On the first day of school we noticed that four of the little girls in the first grade were blind in one or both eyes. They all lived in a specific area of Maranda Tribal Trust Land. At first, Dad thought the blindness might be genetic. But then, he saw that the girls had a tiny white line through their milky-blue lens. Often, I would see them being led in and out of the schoolroom and they would always sit on the front bench (we did not have desks). I spoke to them often, greeting them with the cultural handshake of clasping of hands, clasping of thumbs and clasping of hands in the final shake. They would grasp their left hand to their right elbow in a sign of respect.

Then the girls would lift their heads, turning them slightly as if to focus on our faces, but they had no vision. The girls never missed a day of school and wore their green and white school uniforms proudly.

We attempted to get to know the families and asked questions. Often when examining a patient, Dad found that several stories were told before the real answer came to light. He was very suspicious that he had not heard the *real* story about the circumstances surrounding the girls' blindness.

Then, one night, we woke up to hear our names being called from the road across from the runway. "*Chiremba* (doctor)! *Umfundisi* (teacher) Madame! *Nkoskas* (Miss)!" The voices were urgent. We rushed out the door and saw a family, their heads illuminated by the moonlight. A father wearing tattered khaki shorts and shoes made of old tires and a barefoot mother with a small baby tied to her back and another child in her arms were sitting under a tree at the end of the driveway.

This was where patients came when there was an emergency at night. This couple had walked through the bush for ten miles, the moon barely visible to light the way. I ran ahead and asked what they needed, and they pointed to their six-year-old *chisikana* (little girl). She was holding her hand over her right eye. I removed her hand, and the eye fell out of the socket onto her cheek. The little girl was still, she never cried, not even a whimper. I could feel myself inhaling quantities of air in an effort not to scream. My god, how did something like this happen?

When Dad asked what had happened, the parents said she woke up that way. Then they said the little girl was running and fell on a stick. Then the final story came. The little girl had wakened, crying from a bad dream, and the mother said they must take her to see the *nganga*. During the "consultation," he had said the child was filled

THE POWER OF NGANGA

with evil spirits and that they must come out. With a rusty razor blade, he cut the eye, blinding the little girl. Forever.

Once we realized where the family lived, we connected this to the girls in school. We realized that the *nganga* was personally responsible for all the blindness. Dad immediately sent a message to all the parents to come to a meeting at the school. He explained that for the children to learn to read and get an education, they had to have their eyesight. And if the girls had an education, the parents could command a higher *lobola* (bride-price).

The cutting of the schoolgirls stopped. No confrontation, no ultimatum, only grassroots education about the value associated with sightedness. They understood fully. There were less egregious means for the *nganga* to maintain stature and respect without blinding the children. Evil spirits could be handled by less traumatic means. No struggle of culture against culture—only a slow and gradual adoption of more humane standards of care. But the power of all *ngangas* was deeply entrenched in the culture, regardless of the tribe or social standing in the community.

We hired a husband-and-wife teaching team for the school, Mr. and Mrs. Nkomo. They had gone to college in Bulawayo, had their own vehicle, and traveled frequently back to the city for R&R. Teacher Nkomo, as he preferred to be called and Mrs. Nkomo, as she preferred to be called, were at our home for Sunday tea.

Mrs. Nkomo was petite and reserved and the local community was in awe that she wore a wedding ring, drove a car, and had only one child. Teacher Nkomo was 6'4", elegantly dressed and spoke eloquently and with wisdom. That Sunday afternoon, Dad asked them, "Do you believe in the power of *nganga*?"

Teacher Nkomo stretched his long legs out in front of him and said, "Since you are European, I would say that is absolutely rubbish—of course not. But since we are such close friends, yes, I believe *nganga* can cast a spell on me. He can bewitch me. I will tell you if the *nganga* told me I was to die, I would lay down and die."

Harsh Realities of Bush Living

The *nganga* was not the only cause of physical harm for the African people. Skirmishes with elephants along the Nuanetsi River were common. The animals churned up drinking water in small ponds, turning them into colossal mud pits. In the spring, insects would descend on the elephants, and the elephants would need a daily mud bath to keep the bugs away. They would gouge out holes with their tusks and lower their entire bodies into these depressions. This daily occurrence and competition for water often placed African women in precarious situations.

On one evening, a woman was returning to her village with a tin of water balanced on her head. She was walking down the road to her hut when she encountered a young bull elephant about to cross the road ahead of her.

It was just after sunset. She normally would have stopped and allowed the bull to proceed, but the *doro* (beer) she had consumed that afternoon had deadened her senses and made her less heedful of the danger than normal. She walked on, and when she arrived at the spot where the waiting bull stood, she shouted, "*Voetsak!*" (a word that is Afrikaans in origin and universally means "get away"), just as if a stray or *bundu* dog had offended her.

She was close to the roadside *kraal* where she lived, a matter of two hundred yards — so close that relatives could actually hear her shout. Then they heard horror-stricken screams. Her cries went on for a minute or two, intermingled with the angry trumpeting of the elephant. By the time some men who had been in the maize field some three hundred yards away arrived on the scene, the worst had happened. They found the woman lying in a pool of blood in the center of a tight group of three *mopani* tree trunks, her chest gaping from a tusk wound. The elephant was standing a few feet away from the victim, and when the men shouted and beat on a tin plate with a *knobkerrie* (a club with a rounded head), he turned and grumbled off into the gathering dusk.

The woman's desperate efforts to escape the pursuing bull were plain to see. She had frantically run around in a smallish circle, keeping fairly large trees between her and the relentless pursuer, until in one open space, she must have seen that he was nearly on her, and had darted away to her right. The elephant had braked with such effort that two long gouges in the earth had been left by his thrust-out front feet. He swerved and caught up with her as she crouched in the scanty protection offered by the three-pronged tree. He placed his huge forehead against the trunks and bent them down until one tusk went right through her body and into the soil below.

By chance, I happened to pass this tragic scene on my way home from retrieving the weekly mail, not five minutes after it happened. A couple of men from the village helped me load the woman into the back of the Land Rover. With one hand on the steering wheel, I compressed her hemorrhaging with my other hand — she was already in shock.

I rushed to attempt to get the woman to the clinic. The washed-out roads and riverbeds represented dangerous obstacles; if I dropped a wheel, I'd break an axle. Some places I'd accelerate to 35 mph.

But the 40-mile trip was too far; she bled to death in the Land Rover before I could reach the mission.

Nganga Presents Himself

One of the most profound relationships I developed began while my parents were spending several days in Bulawayo. My brother, Michael, was away at university and I was left to run the mission by myself. I was not yet 17 years old.

Early one morning, I heard a commotion outside. An old man wearing a green, World War II-era British greatcoat approached the house. It was overcast; *guti* (a light misty rain) was lowering the temperature. He was leaning on a *knobkerrie* and was supported by two men on either side.

I didn't recognize any of them. They told me the old man had a burn. I didn't have to pull back the filthy wool coat to know what I'd find — the smell of rotting flesh filled my nostrils. I'd seen so many burns that they usually didn't affect me, but this was the worst I'd seen on a living person. I loaded the three men into the back of the truck and drove them to the clinic. They were facing backwards, legs dangling over the back of the bed of the truck. I eased down the road to the clinic, as the old man was in obvious pain and distress. Instead of taking him inside, I chose to work on him on the wide steps leading up to the clinic.

The stench was unbearable. He'd been burned from his calf to his hip. Maggots were moving freely up and down the five-inch-wide, two-foot-long gaping wound. The burn was so deep I could bury my fingers in his thigh.

Through conversation, I learned the elderly man had rolled into the fire in the middle of his hut while he was sleeping. When I inquired why he had waited so long (two weeks) to seek help, the old man said, "I am Nganga."

A chill came over me. I set my jaw and looked at this old man, without flinching, without showing the fear that was churning in my stomach. I had come face-to-face with the same *nganga* who had used a rusty razor blade to cut out the eyes of the schoolgirls, blinding them, several years before. The *nganga* had used his own *muti* to treat himself. Now his pain and suffering were unbearable. At least he knew enough to recognize it was high time he got help from the mission.

Nganga Samuel and I established a very special relationship. He trusted me implicitly, and during his two-month stay at the clinic, I spent hours with him daily, always respectful of his standing in the community and his stature among the other patients being treated at the clinic.

I would cut away dead skin and Samuel would patiently watch me. One day I asked him to "read the bones" for me. He obliged but would not even take an egg in payment. His reading: "Missy Pa-may-la, you too smart, but you are not studying the books as much as you should." I was shocked. How did he know?

Dad also spent time with the *nganga*, learning about the practice of casting "bones," which were a collection of intricately carved

THE POWER OF NGANGA

Nganga Samuel

wood pieces, bird beaks, and shells. The *nganga* would toss the bones in the air and see how they landed. He would then carefully analyze their placement on the ground to diagnose, counsel, and treat his people.

Our family had been on vacation in neighboring Mozambique and we'd brought home a collection of shells. Dad brought the *nganga* Samuel several and he sorted through them, saying which ones were good for his practice. There was a beautiful inch-long shiny blue shell with a hump in the middle of it among the collection.

The *nganga* pushed that one aside and declared it was no good. Dad looked at him in dismay. "That's my favorite shell." The *nganga* looked at him and asked for an explanation. "It tells whether a woman can become pregnant or not," said Dad. "If the hump lands right side up, she can become pregnant." The two of them laughed. The next day, a line of about 40 women snaked their way single file around the clinic yard. They were waiting for their appointment with the *nganga* and his special hump shell.

As time went on, the bonds between Dad and the *nganga* strengthened. "One day, Nganga said to me, 'Tell me about your God—tell me about the book you read,'" Dad later recalled. "I knew this was the hour for which we had been called."

15
TERRORISM CROSSES ALL BOUNDARIES

My family continued to teach others to carry on our work when the American and European missionaries would be gone. Those who were lifting the cross, helping to carry on, were not all formally educated. As was the case of Chief Maranda, some of the local people wielded significant influence over others.

Political unrest brewing in isolated pockets of the massive Maranda Tribal Trust Land was a source of extreme concern. Several leaders of ZAPU (Zimbabwe African People's Union) and ZANU (Zimbabwe African National Party) were attempting to establish a foothold in the area. Many of them were receiving support, training, and AK-47s from the Chinese government. The Chinese had a history of intolerance toward the Americans and Christian missionaries. A few of the Black rebel leaders had been placed in jail or confined in remote areas by the Rhodesian government to stifle the smoldering unrest.

The people of Maranda, who were for the most part apolitical, were being forced to align with one of these parties without knowing what values or tenets they represented. Within the struggle between the two parties, retaliatory terrorist attacks on opposition villages began, at first like a sluggish puff adder—slow but deadly. As the strikes continued in earnest, the adder developed into an ill-tempered green mamba, viciously attacking without warning.

HOTDOGS FOR HYENAS

Changing sides from one political alliance to another had deadly consequences. One village was attacked because it chose to side with ZAPU. The father, mother, older siblings, and youngest babies were killed, leaving the *mbuya* (grandmother) and two small children ages five and seven.

During the day, the *mbuya* would hide the children in a maize crib. The temperatures hovered around 105 degrees. The dust from the maize and stalks choked the children. The *mbuya* warned them not to cough and begged them not to cry out when they were thirsty. She was trying to save the only two surviving children.

At night, the *mbuya* would hide the children in a hollowed-out baobab tree. In the dark, she would leave the children *sadza* porridge inside the tree. The children were instructed not to move or call for her in the night.

Before the sun came up, she would lead the children back to the maize crib. They would whisper to her, asking when they could go to the river to play, and when they could go to the river to fill the pot with water for cooking. After two months, on a hot, steamy morning, she finally relented. She warned them to be quiet, to play for a short while, and then to return to the village with water.

But the children did not return. She sent a message through a nearby villager, telling Dad to please come to the river and help her find the missing children. I said I would go with him. At first, he shook his head no, then said, "You drive."

We left immediately, fearing the worst. Upon arriving at the banks of the Nuanetsi, we could hear the old woman singing. When we got closer, we saw she had a rusted old shovelhead in her rough, calloused hands. The sharp tip of the shovel was broken off so that the shovel was square across the bottom and nearly rectangular, almost impossible to use for digging in the hardened, drought-stricken dirt. The song she was singing was one we had taught her: "Kana Nzira Yangu Inorugare" ("When Peace like a River").

The old woman, barefoot, clothed in rags, with tears and sweat pouring down her face, was singing! She had found the children

TERRORISM CROSSES ALL BOUNDARIES

brutally murdered. Their body parts were scattered on the banks of the Nuanetsi. She was gathering limbs and heads and trying to bury them. When we dropped to the ground and began to help her, we joined her in song as she arrived at the chorus:

Rugare (rugare),	It is well
Mumwoyo (mumwoyo),	With my soul.
Runyraro mumwoyo wangu.	It is well, it is well, with my soul.

The senseless tribe-on-tribe, black-on-black, opposing political party violence had no purpose. The people were pawns in a deadly international game of chicken. Now, the enemy wasn't ignorance, drought, or famine. The enemy was a century of pent-up misery manifested as political unrest.

16
REENTRY INTO AMERICA

Like most "Third Culture Kids (TCKs)," I struggled with unresolved grief over leaving a country that had defined me (Rhodesia/Zimbabwe) to reenter "America," which was merely my country of birth.

Only thing was, I didn't know it was grief I was experiencing. "Third Culture Kid" wasn't a coined expression in the 1970s. I considered myself to be a Rhodesian who happened to have been born in America. It was just that clear and simple to me.

For lack of a better explanation, I was doing my due diligence, satisfying the wishes of my parents that my higher education would come from a university in the United States. Because of the norm of traveling great distances to get to any destination, none of us grasped how permanent these separations between stable home and values would be.

On the exterior, we Third Culture Kids looked as if we belonged right in the hub of a college campus (in my case Seattle, Washington).

But it would be a very dark period of my life. I was confused about my cultural identity — the life I had been living was normal and now I was a "misfit." What had I done to deserve this? I hadn't even had a voice in the choice.

Even today, saying, "Cheer up, there are a lot of people who have had it worse" doesn't help individuals who have spent their formative years in "third world" cultures. More than likely, we have seen a side of life unknown, forever, to most Americans. And during the most challenging and sometimes terrifying occasions in our life experiences, we have had to reach deep down within ourselves to find a spiritual connection — a place of solace to keep our heads calm. We're pros in that area.

My 1970 reentry into America was traumatic. I boarded the plane in Johannesburg, South Africa on a rainy night. As I sat down in my seat, I sobbed uncontrollably. I knew this was not the right decision for me and I was making the biggest mistake of my life.

I listened to my gut. I unbuckled my seatbelt, threw my Rhodesian-made shoulder bag over my arm and made my way down the aisle to the exit. One of the crew members stopped me and told me I couldn't get off; the doors had already been secured, locked shut.

I sank back into my seat. One kind passenger handed me a drink, and another pushed some white flowers into my hands. I was devastated and simultaneously terrified. I thought my heart would absolutely break into a thousand pieces. And as I stared out the window, the aircraft slipped into the rain-drenched and starless night, stealing me unwillingly out of my Africa.

Culture shock hit me within minutes after I landed at Sea-Tac Airport in Seattle. After I had gone through customs and immigration an African-American skycap picked up my bags, which was okay with me. But what he said startled me. "This way, Ma'am." I was 17. I looked at him with the most incredulous expression. Was it because he said ma'am?

I opened my mouth and said, "You speak English!" I had no idea that Black people spoke English with an American accent. Never in my wildest dreams would I have entertained such a thought. The sky-cap turned to me and smiled.

"Yes, and I work for tips." I had no idea what a tip was. I followed him through the airport. Tip of an iceberg? He's going to give me advice about something? I was clueless. When we got to the waiting area, he stopped, dropped my bags, and spun around to face me.

REENTRY INTO AMERICA

"Thank you ever so much," I said.

The skycap held out his hand, palm side up. Oh, my god, I thought. *That's* what he meant.

I reached in my pockets. I had Swedish kroners, English pounds, French francs, Rhodesian coins. No U.S. money. I'm not even sure I knew what American money looked like. I stuffed some of my international currency into his outstretched hand and took off. I felt like it was Boxing Day (the day after Christmas when gifts and treats are bestowed on employees), only it was August.

Not long after, I was riding with a college classmate to church. He had a white Chevy Bel Air, early 1960s. The car had red leather interior. The guys on campus thought this car was spectacular. We stopped for gas and then he pulled the car towards a small brick building and stopped. I was sitting on the passenger side. The car began to roll forward and I was fine with that until a giant torrent of water enveloped the car. We were now inside a brick building and I was going to drown. I looked at the driver, who was calmly staring straight ahead. I began to panic. Needless to say, this was my first experience of an automatic car wash.

Then my brother, who had preceded me to the same university, put me into a situation that would prove to be humiliating. I had read about demonstrations while I was in Africa. To me this was something I wanted to experience and told him so. We were visiting Portland State University and I spied a group of protesters.

I looked at Mike. "Can I join them?" I asked.

"Sure," he said.

We made our way to the student union center where I got my white cardboard sign with a long handle. Mike and his friends said they'd watch me from the window of the student union. I looked at my sign. "What's gay rights mean?"

Mike grinned. "It means they are really happy. They are demonstrating because they are happy."

That appealed to me. But, of course, once I became a part of the demonstration and heard the yelling and commotion on both sides, I realized there wasn't anything happy about any of it. My brother and his friends were enjoying watching me from the safety of the lounge windows. I, of course, had no idea what the word "gay" meant in America.

It seemed at every turn I made, I experienced culture shock. I was stunned that young men didn't walk on the outside of the sidewalk when walking with me. They talked loud and with little substance in their conversation. I was perplexed—I'd be more honest if I said bored—with their lack of curiosity about the world, people, travel, or domestic and international politics.

I also spoke English with a Rhodesian accent. Fellow students would ask me to speak just to hear my accent. I had to read lips because Americans spoke too fast.

I resolved I would learn to speak just like them. Today, when I'm reading to myself or thinking of words, in my head it is with a Rhodesian accent, but what comes out is American—a "third culture kid" technique. Years later, when I worked for the South African Embassy, I normally answered the phone speaking Afrikaans, my voice pitched an octave higher, normal for women there. It was not unusual for my husband to ask to speak to me. I'd have to identify myself and then proceed in English and the accent he was accustomed to hearing from me in our home.

Will we "third culture kids" share those experiences with you? Probably not. We will relate and tell you the positive sides of our stories. Not until we feel safe and comfortable will we share the troubling times of reentry. If we have lived in politically unstable countries, we probably will not share intimate details with you either at least until there is a feeling of ultimate safety in a relationship with you. And that may never happen.

We are chameleons. We will morph into your world because, well, that is what we TCKs do with ease. In their book *Third Culture Kids: Growing Up Among Worlds*, authors David Pollock and Ruth E. Van Reken have written: "TCKs usually develop some degree of cultural adaptability as a primary tool for surviving the frequent change of

REENTRY INTO AMERICA

cultures. Over and over TCKs use the term chameleons to describe how, after spending a little time observing what is going on, they can easily switch language, style of relating, appearance, and cultural practices to take on the characteristics needed to blend better into the current scene."

I attended the opera shortly after arriving in America. The photo taken of me would never reveal the turmoil that was going on deep inside. My very chic white column gown with the cut out "V" back, mint green velvet belt, and white elbow length gloves was perfect. My long tresses were pulled up into a bun.

I "knew" *Madame Butterfly*. I certainly was not an elitist or a "put on airs" person. I was raised to engage in cultural conversation regardless of my situation, to get to know people. Very European I now realize, but I was stunned that Americans weren't.

I received an instant education in the class "Social Circle 101." Seeing people push themselves into an imaginary spotlight of importance and class, letting their money set boundaries for others, was and still is appalling to me.

Third Culture Kids/Adults (TCK/As) may initially appear to be quiet, but we are often assessing a situation. The reason the opera is still so clear in my memory is that it was the first time I realized I was assessing. And despite my young age as a freshman in college, I was using my cross-cultural skills to figure out the situation.

The new American friends I had made in the arts circle were bantering for social status. That's what they had to offer. They were a superficial commodity. It reminded me of being in the huge tobacco export barns in Africa or the cattle sales where thousands of livestock were being moved to the highest and fastest bidder.

To ease the college transition, my parent's attorney, Marshall Baron, flew from Bulawayo via Israel, London, and Greenwich Village to Seattle for my 18th birthday. We spent several days visiting every art museum and sharing deep, meaningful conversations. I had only been in America for six weeks but I was already starving for the cultural conversation I was not getting from faculty, staff, students, my "newly" found relatives, and my quick immersion into the local congregation.

I was literally drowning. I would fidget during church, "enduring" shallow sermons. The college offered a movie night where *Born Free* was shown. Halfway through I got up sobbing and ran out. The rest of the student body was oohing and aahing over the lions and scenery. This was exotic to them, but home to me.

On campus I visited the dean of women, attempting to explain to her what I was experiencing. She offered no suggestions, no solutions. She was ill equipped to handle what she perceived was a simple case of college freshman homesickness. She didn't get it. There was no home to go to.

And I was not alone. There were five of us Third Culture Kids on campus. We knew each other and even had some of the same classes. But we never opened up with one another. We suffered in silence. We were never considered to be on the same status of international students. After all, we were Americans.

On the other end of the culture shock spectrum was having to do laundry. There were no washers or dryers in the dorm. Students had to trek three blocks up the hill to a laundromat. In Africa, my mum always had a set laundry schedule: Wash on Monday; ironing on Tuesday. She had a Maytag washing machine with a gasoline engine. She cranked out several loads using the same tub of water. After the laundry was run through the wringer, she and Jimius would carry tubs of wet laundry out and hang it on the line in perfect order.

It was not unusual to see them throw netting over the sheets to keep Putzi flies from laying eggs in the seams. If not, the larvae would burrow beneath the skin of the unfortunate sleeper, resulting in itchy skin, boils, and ultimately the maggot itself. Mum always ironed the sheets with an extremely hot iron eliminating the potential of these little buggers attaching themselves to us while we were sleeping.

I never participated in the laundry days. Mum always said there would be plenty of time in my life to take on that duty. Unlike other missionary kids, I *did* know not to mix white and red clothes, but transporting clothes to and from the laundromat was perplexing. I was clueless. I took my laundry basket, hoisted it up on top my head and headed up the hill. That was the only way I'd seen baskets carried. It left my hands free to carry my books. The trip down the hill was the same. Clothes and sheets folded, back in the basket and balanced on my head. I did not know I was to carry the basket in my hands. My way seemed to be far more practical.

When the world is trying to figure out what to do with diversity that is primarily defined by many of the external cultural icebergs, most of us who have been raised in a third culture see the person first—and then the details of race, culture, economic status second, third or maybe not at all.

Many TCK/As approach relationships differently. We value relationships above convenience, as we have lived in far-flung places. It is a gift we carry with us wherever we may go later. We peel away the layers of what makes people tick, we assess relationships on a fast track, and make a determination quickly on what value there is in the relationship. If you pass muster with us, you will have someone in your corner forever. Unconditionally. Regardless of status or income. Check the phone log or social media friends of the TCK. Ask how long you have known the person they're in contact with. You will find it likely stretches decades.

I hadn't thought about the "opera event" for ages until I was at a funeral reception in 2016. Ralph Lloyd of Baltimore, Maryland, whom I had known for all of about thirty minutes, bluntly asked me, "Where do you go when you are with a group of people like this or in other places and their conversation is about their trivial day-to-day problems?"

I attempted to make a joke. "I usually wander to the kitchen and pour a drink or make friends with the family dog."

Ralph pushed me. "No, how do you feel, where do you go inside of yourself when you get surrounded with superficiality and you've experienced real world problems and tragedies?"

I joked with Ralph and told him to get out of my head but went on to thank him because he was the first person to have ever asked me these questions.

He was observing the observer. I had to digest what he was asking, and he wanted an answer. Finally, I said, "I guess I engage *dis*engage."

Ralph said, "Okay, so you politely listen and you're thinking to yourself, 'You haven't seen anything and you don't know how lucky you are.'"

At this point Ralph and I were sitting in living room chairs facing each other. I was feeling a little uncomfortable because he was not going to let go until getting an honest answer from me. I decided I couldn't make an excuse to get a drink or find the family dog. Ralph's brother John, who was sitting on the other side of me said in his ever-diplomatic way, "Maybe you're pushing a button she doesn't want pushed."

I thought for a moment and decided to charge ahead. "Ralph, you are right," I said. "I often listen to conversations, trying to remember they are 'cocktail conversations' and while I'm shaking my head in agreement of someone's superficial plight, my head is thinking of malnutrition-riddled two-year-olds who are so weak, their cries are barely audible. They open their mouths, and no sound comes out. I look at the person who is complaining, who clearly has the vocal cords to be heard over a crowd, and I think of a little child with reddish hair, laying on his mother's lap on a dirty white tattered blanket, starving. And while I understand perception, I am thinking to myself as I converse with the person in the crowd, you have no idea how blessed your life is."

Annoyed, I made eye contact with Ralph. "No, I didn't really want to answer your question."

"Good," said Ralph. "I knew if I pushed you, you would. You have something to say. Maybe you need to be more open."

I laughed sarcastically. "Right," I said.

However, what he said made me think. A few months later, Dad and then another friend of mine from South Carolina called. The conversations both shifted to some dire "need" of someone who was going through a crisis. Instead of saying, "Uh, hunh, oh that's too bad," I became agitated and felt like my time was being wasted. But I reeled myself in. I started asking basic questions using Maslow's Hierarchy of Needs. By the time I was finished. I said, "Next time you talk to this person, ask them basic questions. Then tell them how fortunate they are."

Ralph hadn't opened Pandora's box, but he made me think that my silence wasn't always helpful and if I used my cultural skills diplomatically, I could make tiny changes.

During a conference I attended in Kentucky in 2016, fifteen of us Third Culture (mission) Kids locked ourselves away from significant others to share our stories. Our reentry into America was one of a singular voice. Our observations and struggles were felt by everyone in the room. And although we had known each other as children, we all thought our grief of losing a sense of place, our families, our standards, our homes, siblings, family dogs, friends, familiar foods, language, a connection with nature was an individual phenomenon. We thought we were all alone.

Interestingly, statistics show that children of missionaries do well academically. A survey of 608 adult missionary kids conducted by MKCART/CORE (a research organization composed of ten mission agencies) results in these startling statistics.

- 30 percent of the respondents graduated from high school *with honors*
- 27 percent were elected to the National Honor Society
- 94 percent went on to university-level studies
- 73 percent graduated from university
- 25 percent graduated from university *with honors*
- 3 percent were Phi Beta Kappas
- 11 percent were listed in *Who's Who in American Colleges and Universities*

My longtime friend and fellow TCK/A, Dr. Alan Smith and me playing a song at a conference.

Another survey on TCK/As (Adult Third Culture Kids) confirms that a strikingly high percent of TCKs go onto post-secondary education. In 1993, a study of 680 TCK/As conducted by John and Ruth Hill Useem and their colleagues showed that while only 21 percent of the U.S. population as a whole has graduated from a four-year college or university, 81 percent of the TCK/As they surveyed had earned at least a bachelor's degree. Half of them went onto earn master's or doctorate degrees. (Useem & Useem, 1996) When the fifteen of us mission kids met in 2016, we found that only one had stopped with an undergraduate degree. The other fourteen had at least a master's degree. Four were medical doctors.

Lessons Learned

A recent study of Third Culture Adults has found that we use our cultural experiences well and learn there is always a reason behind anyone's behavior, no matter how mystifying it appears. We are usually more patient than others in a particular situation to try to understand what's going on.

Cultural adaptability may initially be used as a survival tool, but it has incredible benefits. TCK/As normally adjust with relative calm to life where meetings may start the exact minute for which they have been scheduled or two hours later, depending on which country they're in. Partly because of the frequency with which we have traveled and moved, we are known to roll with the punches, even in the most unusual circumstances. And, while it is a strange place to give thanks, I want to thank the individuals throughout my career that told me to "dumb down my resume." I thank the professor at Catholic University who called me in for a consult to ask, "Did your husband take your exam? No woman could have scored so high. It looks like the president of GE has taken this." And thank you to the president of the company who made sexual advances towards me on a business trip and because I told him to, "Go take a cold shower," promptly fired me upon my return to Washington, D.C. (I could not file suit because it would have impacted my then active-duty husband's military career.)

Those very personal and difficult lessons instilled in me the wisdom from my father that: "The pendulum swings both ways." Never during all my opportunities and experiences in Africa would I have dreamed that in America, I would encounter derogatory remarks and actions.

So how does healing occur for the Adult Third Culture Kid? Obviously, our parents cannot go back and undo the transitional or separation experiences. The years of family life lost are irretrievable.

In fact, most TCK/As cannot recover their hidden losses. We can't reclaim the sights, sounds, or smells that made home "home" as a child. We can't stop the war that displaced us or whatever our relocation circumstances were.

What we *can* do, however, is to learn to put words to our past, name our experiences, validate the benefits as well as the losses, and ask for help when needed. We can learn to name the gifts we have been given and that we are often unconsciously using them productively.

I found selecting mates has been painful. And I settled in my relationships to the point, a former partner told me I had settled even with him. It has been extremely difficult to find someone that brings balance. I found that if someone matched my intellectual curiosity, they had no experience with basic skills, and if someone had basic skills, there were no other boxes in our relationship that could be ticked off.

My dad had a catch phrase. "Let me show you how to weld, work on a diesel engine, change a spark plug." And this always ended with, "In case you marry someone stupid." It became a joke. Whenever he wanted to teach me how to do something, I would laughingly finish the reason behind his tutelage. Even though I have been expected to perform at a high level, at the end of the day, I'm still a woman who craves intimacy, both giving and receiving.

And finally, TCKs carry the cultural norms they are raised with, often not realizing that it may not be the norm in their birth country. When I was 16, Dad felt it was time to help him in a delivery. It wasn't that he really needed my help — he wanted to impress upon me that bringing children into the world shouldn't be a spur of the moment decision. Since this was the mother's first delivery we settled in for a long night. The young mother chatted with us and when the time was closer for delivery, she climbed up on the table. She pushed when she was told. Never cried out or used any one's name in vain. There was no panting, choo-chooing – just well collected breathing.

The event was quiet and dignified. She needed an episiotomy. That was quick and the baby came straight out into my hands. Before you think this was an emotionless event, let me say that tears rolled down her cheeks when I laid her baby son in the crook of her arm. After a few moments of rest, the mother swung her legs off the table and walked out of the room with her own mother, the baby in her arms.

Walking home that night. Dad said, "Well, what did you think?" I was silent for a few seconds then said, "It was pretty cool."

At the next delivery, I took over a Pepsi and freshly-baked gingerbread and placed it at the end of the delivery table (remember I was 16), chatted with the soon-to-be mom, and informed Dad when she was close to delivery. All the births I was fortunate to assist in were filled with calm — even when an emergency arose. That was how I observed it was supposed to be.

Over a decade later, before I delivered my own son Thomas, I watered my plants first and arrived at the hospital in heels with the Sunday *Washington Post* under my arm. I had this.

Within a short period of time, women in rooms on either side of me were yelling and screaming. I was getting off the bed, when the nurse came in and asked me where I thought I was going. "I can't focus with all that noise," I said. "I need to shut my door."

I had no idea I was to be vocal during childbirth. Upon administering Pitocin, the staff explained that the contractions would come on hard and fast. They did, but I never connected the dots that I should be vocal as I was hearing from other mothers throughout the floor. I had a new small paint roller in my bag. I asked the young resident doctor if he could hand it to me for my back labor. That worked beautifully.

In the end, I needed an emergency C-section and the attempt to administer the epidural failed. My son was in fetal distress. With great urgency they told me to breathe through the operation. I focused on the overhead light and they hurriedly made an incision — so quickly they cut my son's neck with the scalpel.

My cultural understanding of birth with dignity and quiet was evaporating. After they rushed him to the NICU, I asked how soon I could see him. Not thinking I'd attempt to get out of the bed the nurse said, "Honey, you will have to scrub first."

I gathered my gown around me as dignified as I could, swung my feet off the bed and eased down to the floor. "Where do I scrub?" I asked.

Shortly after that my parents called the hospital from Botswana. They identified themselves and Dad asked to speak to me. The floor nurse told him, "We're not sure she can get to the phone. She's just had a Caesarean, you know."

Dad chuckled and said, "She's from Africa, you know."

I got on the phone.

17
ATTACK ON MY MOTHER

In the mid-1970s my parents, forced to leave Zimbabwe because of Central Africa Mission, purchased a 10,000-acre farm in neighboring Botswana. Land was fairly cheap in this area and this tract was considered a farm, not a ranch. Because of droughts, 25 acres per head of cattle was considered the norm for sustainability.

Close to an area known as the Tuli Block, the farm was nestled in the corner of Zimbabwe, South Africa and Botswana. The farm was laid out near the southern banks of the Limpopo River on the Botswana side, but they had an Alldays, South Africa, address. Alldays was a small town of about 3,000 with the Venetia diamond mine close by.

Starting over for them, now in their 50s, was tough, but Dad was determined to build a new place for Mum, a place where she could once again grow beautiful gardens. After leaving Rhodesia, she told him she thought she'd never have her own home again. He was going to turn the sadness of the losses of Rhodesia into a dream come true in Botswana.

The biggest problem they had in establishing the new farm were the elephants. Fencing would be strung to cross section the land. That same night, the roving elephants would trample and destroy the fencing to get to delectable trees for midnight grazing. While I was living in Europe, I delighted in reading their escapades and challenges with the "eles." The damage they inflicted on trees and fencing was horrendous, but I couldn't help but find the calamitous recitations humorous. The elephants were there first—the landscape belonged to them; man came a long time afterward.

Now, Dad wanted me to come home. They were in a safe place. He had dreams of building a safari ranch and wanted me to assume the role of ferry pilot, picking up guests in Jo-burg and flying them into Botswana. It was oh, so tempting, but while living in Europe, I had met an Army colonel and fallen in love, and we were making plans for our future together. I asked my soon-to-be husband if he was interested in settling in Africa. He was well-read on Africa's politics, coups, and government corruption. His response? "Hell no. I served in Vietnam. I intend to keep you safe."

Dad left Mum at the farm on a Saturday morning in June 1979, to pick up supplies in Pietersburg (now Polokwane), South Africa, 150 miles away. Dad said, "I kissed her goodbye and asked what she planned to fix for dinner. Not that the menu was important. I wanted to tease her to see how she'd respond."

Mum, knowing how he would rather have dessert before dinner, replied, "Tonight you're getting nothing but spinach." Dad had been made to eat spinach as a young boy, and the only meal request he had made when they started their family was that their children would never be forced to eat spinach. Dad started to open his mouth in protest. Mum continued, "You forgot that agreement was good only when the children were with us." With a smile, she waved at him and walked back into her kitchen.

Dad felt comfortable leaving Mum alone. Amon, their trusted houseboy and gardener, had been with the family for over ten years and was considered reliable, but Mum always kept the gun safe locked when he cleaned the bedroom. The Rhodesian Bush War was then in its fourteenth year. Even though they had moved across the border, there was an easily crossable river that separated the two countries.

Amon, who worked only half days on Saturday, raised his hand to stop Dad as he was leaving. "Baas," he said, "I am planning to

ATTACK ON MY MOTHER

make a trip to see my family soon." Dad smiled but thought that was an odd statement. Why did Amon want to have this conversation with him now? He needed to drive across the border, get supplies and return before nightfall. Dad knew that by the time he arrived home, Mum would have had a bath, fixed her hair, and put a crisply ironed dress on. After thirty-five years of marriage, she was still his bride.

My Doberman, *Bietjie* (little beast in Afrikaans), dutifully followed Mum from room to room, often stretching himself across a door threshold to guard her. While not the brightest canine in the world, he appeared, as most Dobermans, extremely menacing. He was a warm chocolate color with tan points. His ears had been left natural, but his tail was docked.

Most stores in Africa allowed dogs on their premises. When Bietjie sauntered in with his choke-chain collar, patrons would clear a path for him. Today, all Bietjie wanted to do was jump in the Land Rover and go.

"Not today, old man," said Dad. "Stay here and watch Mommy."

The border police and customs officers at Botswana were notoriously crooked. If they were not given a bribe, they would go through the toolboxes and scatter wrenches, sockets, and screwdrivers on the road, pretending they were looking for items that should be declared. Mum had found they liked bread. She piled two loaves of bread into Dad's arms before he left. Now the border officials happily waved him through, thanked him for the bread, and his toolboxes remained intact. He made his way into South Africa.

But soon, Dad would be hit to his core with a powerful word he had "drilled" (his term) into all of us: resilience.

At noon, Amon prepared to leave and he stopped to say *chisarai* (I am leaving, but you are staying here), a common way of saying goodbye in the Shona language. Mum paid him and watched him shuffle down the road, cash wages stuffed in his pocket. She smiled to herself and wondered whether the money would make it across the river to feed his family or be intercepted by one of the local prostitutes. An account of the event, following a police investigation, was later revealed to our family.

Amon walked alone down the sandy road, singing to himself. He stopped in at the local, fly-infested, one-room store.

One of the belligerent drunks in the store grumbled, "Iwe!" (You!)

Amon turned around and said, "*Masakati* (Good afternoon)."

The drunk said, "When is Chiremba returning?" referring to Dad.

Amon took a short breath. "Madame did not say."

Those words were the signal. They knew Madame was alone. Amon had just become Mum's Judas Iscariot.

Six thugs who had been sitting outside the store ambled inside and walked straight back to the storeroom. The storekeeper didn't even look up. The local tailor and dressmaker kept his head bent over the treadle sewing machine. His feet went faster in a vain attempt to drown out the coded conversation. Within minutes, the thugs walked out, each carrying an AK-47. A small baby strapped to her mother's back started to cry. The mother quickly hushed the baby with her breast as she looked over the storekeeper's dusty tins of food.

The sun was setting when Mum walked to the generator shed to start the 5 KVA generator, which provided dependable electric power for the homestead. She checked to make sure it was turned from kerosene fuel to petrol for easy starting and grabbed the crank handle. With a strong pull, the generator sprang to life, first with a few irregular sputters and then with a solid, steady chugging sound. She then turned the generator back over to the cheaper and more plentiful kerosene, shut the generator-shed door, and headed for the house. Bietjie followed closely behind.

In anticipation of Dad's return, Mum began to prepare dinner. Dad was a meat-and-potatoes kind of guy who still enjoyed a four-course meal at dinner. While Mum was in the kitchen, Bietjie jumped to attention and began to growl. He peered out the window, his fangs exposed. Mum looked out over the massive canine and saw a woman approaching with a baby on her back. Mum recognized this woman as a regular at the store.

ATTACK ON MY MOTHER

The woman said, "Madame, my baby is sick. She needs *muti* (medicine)."

Mum asked, "Where is she sick?"

"*Matumbu*," was all the woman said. That was a catchall word to describe stomach ailments that could mean anything from syphilis to diarrhea.

Mum told the mother to take the baby out of the sling. She walked back into the house to get her medical supplies, Bietjie once again on her heels. Since Mum seemed calm, the guard dog in Bietjie seemed to accept the intruder too.

As she gathered some essentials, Mum glanced at the side arm by the bed. She started to reach for it and put it with her supplies, but she stopped. The neighborhood had been quiet, with no acts of terrorism for quite a while.

"Let's not be too anxious," she thought to herself. Dad would be home before nightfall. She wasn't afraid to be by herself. Then again, there was a war going on, and they'd lost several friends in brutal isolated attacks.

Mum carefully knelt and began to examine the infant. The baby's hair was already turning red, and her belly was distended, all signs of advanced malnutrition. Mum asked the mother whether she had enough milk.

"*Handizivi*, I don't know," replied the mother.

Mum knew that milk was allegedly provided by the government, but much was diverted, and the "free" supplies often came at a premium. Mum asked again, and the mother confessed that she had no milk for the child and was giving the baby only water from the river.

Mum knew this water was contaminated with numerous microorganisms, from amoebas to giardia all the way to larger worms. On the bacterial front, typhoid, *E. coli*, salmonella, and shigella often appeared at epidemic levels. Cholera outbreaks could decimate entire villages. Sanitation was nonexistent, and urine and fecal material ran straight to the river, which provided the only source of water in the drought-stricken region. To treat the water to make it potable was impractical—there was not enough energy to boil it, there was insufficient chlorine or chemicals to treat it, and there were very few storage facilities to hold clean water.

Lack of clean water was and is a major obstacle to improving life expectancy in Africa. Millions still die from water-related illnesses every year. Dad had just completed building large concrete holding tanks, laid down pipe from the river and was pumping enough water for the local people to finally have a safe supply for drinking water.

Just as Mum was thinking proudly about what her husband had achieved in creating safe water for his community, out of nowhere a series of rapid pops filled the air.

Bietjie yelped just as Mum turned her head. The beloved dog made one final lunge at the first of the thugs bursting through the open door. The weapon was already turned to the floor; little motion was necessary to take down the dog in midair as Bietjie leapt to protect his mistress. The dog hit the ground with a thud.

Mum felt the baby being abruptly jerked out of her comforting arms and realized that the woman and her sick baby had been a decoy. They had intended to distract her during these daylight hours.

Mum refused to show fear or scream as a knife was held to her throat. She quietly prayed as she was forced outside and bound to a tree. The brutality of their efforts to destroy her faith and crush her love for this primitive corner of God's creation was slow and intentional *schadenfreude*. The fierce abuse was meted out in succession until Mum was no longer able to stand. Tied to the tree, she had no means to resist. She could only slump; she couldn't fall. Why they didn't murder the body just as they had attempted to kill her spirit, we will never know.

This African paradise had instantly become hell on earth. As they departed with most of the family's limited possessions, they gave her a push, letting her near-lifeless body fall to the ground, leaving her for dead.

Meanwhile, Dad was anxious to get back to share with Mum news of "the outside world." It had been another day with perfect African

ATTACK ON MY MOTHER

weather. Soon the brilliant orange sun would be streaming dusty rays through the acacia trees before exploding into a spectacular sunset, the kind that can be experienced only in southern Africa. On his way, he spotted a herd of zebra and wildebeest on their nightly migration to the nearby dam for water— the beauty of Africa at its most majestic at twilight.

But when Dad pulled into the homestead, he knew immediately that something was wrong. Where was Fran? Bietjie's keen sense of hearing would usually alert everyone Dad was on his way home. Mum was always there as he rolled up. Now there was no Fran. No Bietjie.

He jumped out without closing the door, and began to run toward the house, calling Fran's name. His anxiety increased with every step, and he reached for his sidearm. The .45 was out of the holster and was cocked before he reached the side of the house. The primeval scream he emitted when he encountered her nearly lifeless body crumpled in the front yard will forever be etched in the annals of time.

He found Mum on the ground, still partially tied to a tree. As she grabbed her chest, he thought she was suffering a heart attack; then he realized she was trying to talk. She said, "They took my typewriter and the Revere Ware." (A treasured wedding gift they had received in 1944). Regardless of where we were, Mum scrubbed the copper bottoms of these pots after each usage until they glistened like new.

Dad still didn't understand what Mum was trying to mouth to him. Her face was dirty, stained with tears, her lips bleeding. He scooped her up in his arms and began running to the bedroom with her. He needed to get her off the ground. He needed to save her. As he approached the front steps, he spotted Bietjie's body. Several rounds had exited the beautiful brown and tan dog's shoulder.

Dad deduced that terrorists from outside the area had attacked Mum, tied her to a tree, raped her, and left her for dead. The woman he considered the strongest person he'd ever known, who insisted on attending to his needs before he knew they were needs, the woman who loved the people of Africa and was loved and respected by everyone, was limp in his arms. The accumulated joys filling a quarter century dedicated to bringing the Word to a primitive people were erased in an instant. Utopia had become hell.

No matter how pure the intentions and how deep the love for others, Dad was now defeated. He had successfully protected his family from unimaginable dangers only to confront his ultimate failure. What self-respecting man could allow such to befall his beloved?

Word soon reached me and my brother Michael about the tragedy. I was working at the South African Embassy in Washington, D.C. On the Monday morning after the attack, the head of South African intelligence at the embassy received news of Mum's attack and notified the ambassador. I arrived at work that morning and pulled into the rear parking lot. We were right next door to the Iranian embassy and because of the volatile situation in the Middle East, we no longer parked on the street, finding it preferable to park behind our building.

As I walked in the door, I was immediately called to the ambassador's office. As I walked into the elevator and punched the third-floor button, I thought it odd an unscheduled meeting was being held. My eyes swept around Ambassador Botha's office. He wasn't alone. The charge d'affaires and several other officers and secretaries were all standing.

Normally, tea wasn't served until 9:30, but it was 8:30, and the tea trolley was filled. Someone handed me a cup and asked me to sit down. With the serious issues of security and violence with the Persian/Iranian embassy next door, I thought that's where the meeting was headed. I had had lunch with a Zimbabwean "official" at the International Monetary Fund who had asked whether my office had bulletproof windows. I had immediately reported this to the embassy security. Now what?

It had been forty-eight hours since the attack on Mum. Ambassador Botha filled me in on every known detail. My index finger was tightly locked through my teacup. The news had swept through the building and co-workers were as stunned as I was. "I'm so terribly sorry" was spoken to me over and over.

ATTACK ON MY MOTHER

Mum had been able to identify the terrorists' origin because of the *Chikaranga* dialect they spoke to one another. With that information, they knew the attackers were from the Rhodesian side. But why her? I was eight months pregnant with my first child, so it was unadvisable for me to return to Africa. However, Michael, who was on the West Coast, boarded a flight immediately.

Dad had taken Mum to Pietersburg, South Africa, to recuperate at their apartment and wait for Michael's arrival. Once Michael landed and picked up his baggage, he drove directly to the apartment to see the folks. After he'd spoken with them, he drove across the border to the farm in Botswana. When he stepped out of the Land Rover, he looked down at the mourning doves scurrying around the road. That was when he saw the spent AK-47 shells by his feet. The casings seemed larger than he had remembered.

A wave of nausea rolled up from his stomach. He cried and vomited simultaneously. This was his home, his Africa, his mother, who was everything to him.

He'd seen enough. He immediately got in the Land Rover and drove back to town. Mike strongly recommended to Mum and Dad that they all return to the United States for rest, but Dad and Mum were committed to the people of Africa. They had wanted to stay until God closed all the doors. Perhaps this was the final door.

They were financially ruined, broke. They were using credit cards to pay subsistence expenses, even to pay for their flight back to the States. The lawsuit with Central Africa Mission had devastated them physically and financially. They needed to regain their strength. Their only remaining possession was an unmovable faith in God.

As they packed, they placed their worn Bible on top of their belongings. It would be the first thing they unpacked in America. While they were clearing customs at Dulles International Airport in Virginia, I waited in baggage and spotted my parents through a partition and gasped. My well-collected mum had aged prematurely. I fought back the tears as I squeezed my son, Thomas, in my arms.

Mum brightened up as soon as she saw me. I placed my son in her arms so she could feel how vibrant life was once more. Several days later I was walking down the hall to the guest room where my parents were staying. My mother was sitting cross-legged on the floor weeping, her Bible in her lap. Respecting the intense privacy she had always practiced, I slipped back down the hall. I have wished so many times I would have overstepped my boundaries, hugging her, and letting her know she was safe and deeply loved.

Upon my parents' arrival back in the States, the colleagues, friends and supporters my family previously had relied on all immediately turned their backs on them. Doors that were once opened to Dad, particularly on speaking circuits, were now closed to this inspiring and inspired orator.

Hearing the truth about my parents' horrendous ordeal, Dr. Jerry Falwell reached out to Dad, asking him to speak at Thomas Road Baptist Church in Lynchburg, Virginia, Falwell's home church. They forged a friendship, spending hours conversing on the indomitable powers of the Holy Spirit.

Falwell urged Mum and Dad to settle in Lynchburg as an opportunity to restore their minds, bodies, and souls. He initiated an open-door policy, facilitating speaking engagements for Dad across America. They lived for nearly two years in Lynchburg, and the family ties continued to strengthen. The spiritual bonds and deep commitment to spreading the Word were immutable and served as salvation for this abused couple who was now embarking on a long and slow recovery.

18
GOING BACK HOME TO VISIT

In 2001, I was asked to be a member of an NGO team heading to South Africa for the UN Conference on Racism. I was working for Lenoir-Rhyne University as the director of several race grant initiatives. Z. Smith Reynolds one of my grantors, was ecstatic and urged me to take advantage of this opportunity. Race Will Not Divide Us was one of Z. Smith Reynolds' projects and I was a natural to fulfill all the boxes, both locally and internationally.

I sat down and talked to the president of the college. "Suppose something dreadful happens over there?" he asked. "It would look bad for the college."

I reflected for a minute thinking he never expressed concern for my safety or the fact I was leaving my young daughter stateside where I would have limited email usage. Fortunately, the academic dean, every chair at the college, the mayor of Hickory, the local leaders in government and business, and my board members tilted the scales, embracing the mission 100 percent. I also asked if I could take an undergrad with me. That was approved as well, and her expenses were met.

Before I left for Africa, I asked my daughter, Summer Brook, "What would you like mommy to bring you from Africa?" Thinking she would ask for a stuffed animal or a necklace, I was stunned when she responded, "A puppy." Quite the order from a six-year old.

HOTDOGS FOR HYENAS

My student and I boarded the 24-hour flight on an overcrowded 747. Everyone on board was heading to the Conference. I saw faces I'd only read about—leaders from the Civil Rights Movement, actors (Tavis Smiley) and activists (Angela Davis). When we arrived in Durban, South Africa, one of the African-American passengers who had brought her young teenage son along announced, "Kiss the ground, we've come home."

I pushed my luggage around the two of them, thinking, "You haven't a clue about Africa. You don't know the cultures, any of the sixteen official languages of South Africa, what the food tastes like or how children are raised and expected to conduct themselves in school. *I'm* the one who's come home."

On the trip over, I clued in my undergrad student about petty theft, to never to get into a white van—even if you think it's a taxi (a sector of Nigerians had inundated South Africa in sex trafficking using white vans)—and how not to be the "ugly American."

I rented a car at the airport. The sun was glaring hot and every car in the parking lot as well as a good portion of cars in Africa are white. We finally found our white VW and headed for friends of mine who had a B&B. The student looked at me in terror when I pulled out onto the left side of the road. She screamed and pushed her feet straight out.

I grinned. It was good to be driving on the "correct" side of the road. I wasn't sure what the speed limit was, so I asked her to look out for the next speed sign. She said, "How do you know which one is the right sign?"

"It's round and has a number in the middle of it." I responded.

She spotted the next little round sign: "120" she read out. Then she looked at me. "OH, MY GOD!" she yelled. "We're gonna die."

"That's kilometers, not miles per hour," I assured her. "But fasten your seatbelt. You won't find Southern gentility here behind the wheel."

Before being mired in the conference, I took my student shopping, teaching her the art of bartering in an open-air market. I didn't hover—I wanted her to get immersed in the culture—so I moved down to the next stall. I'd eyed a chess set with carved Zulu warriors as the pieces that was screaming my name.

A little while later she said she needed to go to the ATM. I raised my eyebrows. "What happened to your cash? Show me how you are buying things."

She had her eye on some carved elephants. I followed her over. "Hey whatsup?" she asked. "I see we're dressed alike. Lemme ax you where y'all got your head wrap from?"

"How much you want for those things right there?"

I pulled her aside. "What are you doing?" We had just gone through Barter Charm School 101.

"Well," she said, "I want them to recognize that my people are from Africa too."

I frowned. "She doesn't see color or your wrap. All she sees and hears is you are a naïve American with cash spilling out of your bag."

From that point forward, the shopping went well. She got the souvenir treasures she wanted, but my baby-sitting nightmare with her was to begin in a few days. She met up with some "diplomats" who invited her out. She didn't tell me or our hosts where she was going and with whom. She crawled into their white van and they took her out drinking. When she didn't arrive at the B&B for dinner we were alarmed. She didn't have her passport on her for ID. We found it in her room. Our hosts called the police. They were overwhelmed with a city that was bulging with foreigners.

Finally, she came in around 2 a.m. She'd gotten free and hailed a cab. She didn't even know the address of the B&B. Thankfully, the taxi driver knew the area and delivered her to us.

The opening of the conference was held in a cricket stadium in Durban. I'd been given a press pass, which I knew would be a great advantage to get some spectacular photos. Shortly after all the introductions, I turned around and saw a chilling banner in white with red letters. "Beware President Bush, blood will be on your hands." It made me feel very uncomfortable.

Later, at the Hilton Hotel at the youth conference, a group of outspoken Muslim youths were blocking the exits to the downstairs reception areas and front doors. I'd spotted them earlier sitting on a back row, engrossed not in the conference, but in conversation. TV cameras were rolling, attempting to get the best news stories to release. The youths shared one keffiyeh, pulling it over their heads as the reporter would ask them a question. It would have been comical because the TV viewers would have thought they all had their own head scarves, not one. They screamed to be heard about the injustices of the United States.

I said to my student, "This is a great place for a bomb to go off right now. Let's seriously find a stairwell and get out of here."

Noticeably absent from the conference were United States government officials. During Fidel Castro's and Yasser Arafat's speeches, Castro said, "Ahh...and where are the Americans? They simply did not show up?"

Castro, even though he spoke through an interpreter, was engaging and animated. He twisted and turned his hands for emphasis when he asked where the Americans were. He was nothing like I had imagined. Remember that my understanding of him was centered on the training of terrorists in Africa and the resulting deadly outcomes. At the conference, I was within a few feet of this leader who presented himself as outgoing and pleasant.

Outside of the conference area there were cartoons of Secretary of State Colin Powell plastered everywhere—pointing out the absence of America at this important UN Conference. I heard that the only other country not in

GOING BACK HOME TO VISIT

attendance was Zimbabwe and that was because President Robert Mugabe was not welcome.

A week into the conference, I slipped away and flew up to Nelspruit to spend time at Kruger National Park. My high school sweetheart Trevor (of impala hunting/croc watching days) met me and we spent a couple days in the park, giving me the opportunity to breathe the air of the bush and to feast upon *boerewors* and *biltong*. The splendor of Africa had not diminished one iota.

Once back in Durban, the political atmosphere was still disturbing. We could feel something was going to happen, but not sure what it was. I visited a primary school as part of a partnership with an elementary school in North Carolina. When I arrived, I had to be let into the gated and locked parking lot for teachers. At the front door, another locked door and the teacher's lounge had a coded access for entry. The after-school day care had bars on the doors and windows.

That day the school was having a silent protest and they invited me to watch. A local judge had been murdered in his front yard, blocks from the school, by a terrorist. The students dressed solemnly in their green school uniforms— students of all races and languages holding signs stating, "Stop the Killing." I was in awe that children in the

third grade understood the depths of terrorism and how they were protected under lock and key every day at their school.

At the end of the day, I said to the teachers, "Our schools in America are not like this."

One of them responded, "Welcome to our world. You Yanks have been lucky not to have been touched by terrorism."

The date was Friday, September 7, 2001.

HOTDOGS for HYENAS

Third grader demonstrating against violence after a judge was killed blocks away from the school.

Between conference sessions, I had located a puppy for my daughter. My host and I decided to drive out one night and take a look at her. Because of car-jackings, they recommended we not take their Mercedes, but my Volkswagen. There was one corner that was notorious for car-jackings and we sped around it even though the light was red. When we got to the next light, it was red as well. A car was stopped at the light with its flashers on. Dave, my host, said, "This could be a trap, we can't stop." And he swerved around the car and the red light.

We arrived at the home where the puppy was, and I fell instantly in love. She was a Rhodesian Ridgeback/Boerbol cross. I named her Shumba, paid them cash and began the arrangement to have her flown to America once she was old enough to have her rabies shot.

Back at the UN Conference and conference grounds, the air of something ominous continued brewing. I said to my student, "I think we need to leave early and get a flight back to the U.S. Something is about to happen, and I don't think we need to be stranded overseas." On top of it all, I was not feeling well. I'd had enough bouts of reoccurring malaria to know what the warning symptoms were. The little "mossies" even welcomed me home one night. I'd had the window open and a few mosquitos were using me for target practice. Their whining was incessant. I finally crawled out of bed, threw a tea service net weighted on the edges with beads over my face and went back to bed.

We left Durban and arrived in Jo-burg and it was evident we weren't the only ones who were trying to catch early flights out. It

GOING BACK HOME TO VISIT

looked like a cattle call. I said to the student, "Take my laptop. I've got all the Castro and Arafat interviews on it. I'll get the next plane out." Somehow, I managed to get on the same flight, but I was feeling quite ill. We arrived back in America not only jetlagged, but my malaria flare was in full force. It was now September 10.

The next morning, I agreed to go on a field trip with my daughter. Feeling absolutely wretched, I was able to get another mother to drive me. I had my head leaning against the dashboard. It was boiling hot out, but I had a sweater on. Suddenly, the radio blared out that the Twin Towers in New York had been destroyed. We proceeded on the field trip to the zoo. Outside there was a sign that said if anyone had been exposed to hoof and mouth disease, they could not come in. I'd just come from Kruger National Park and the bush and yes, there was no doubt hoof and mouth disease there. I collapsed on a bench outside and took a nap.

The airports were closed internationally. What to do about this adorable puppy I couldn't get out of South Africa and into the U.S.? After two weeks, air travel resumed. I received a call from Gatwick Airport in the U.K. Could I get the dog out now?

"Why?" I asked.

Within a half hour, I had an answer. "Well, we're about to bomb Afghanistan." Shumba was on the next flight out of Durban, South Africa, bound for her new home in North Carolina. After a few days rest, I returned to work at Lenoir-Rhyne to find disturbing information. All of the programs and inter-working relationships we had planned to accomplish between universities and schools in South Africa and the U.S. had been extinguished in the after effects of 9/11. No one had time for virtual classrooms or international projects. The U.S. was now suddenly consumed with terrorism and isolationism.

The hopes of educators in Africa connecting with colleagues in America were dashed. The enthusiasm multicultural students of Africa were looking forward to sharing with American students was forever dimmed. In less than a week, our schools in America took on the same persona I had looked at with such disdain in my beloved Africa.

But this unexpected outcome was fine for the plans the college had. The grants we worked so hard to develop, hoping to bring Lenoir-Rhyne to the forefront in making changes in our community regarding racism and social justice, went out the window. When a Charlotte, North Carolina television station contacted me to interview me, students and faculty, and film the campus, I included the academic dean in this request. Instead of putting us on the map, he said, "Have them go down to the athletic center if they want to film diversity."

I forged ahead. A year after my return from Africa, I was able to secure an unused middle school building in close proximity to the campus. There I was able to house Centro Latino, The United Hmong Association, The Umoja Dance Team, The Native American Association and our coordinating program. While the school enjoyed the grant funding and the prestige of exposure, they were not interested in any programs that were sustainable. Matter of fact, the Martin Luther King Day Walk was sufficient to them. Lenoir-Rhyne made sure though there was transportation waiting for the students at the African-American sports center to whisk them back to campus when the walk across the railroad tracks was over.

During this time, when we asked for documentation from the administration regarding where some of the funding was going, the return emails were filled with capital letters, screaming that my request was completely unprofessional.

I uncovered a salary being paid to a non-employee through our grant money. I immediately investigated this line item and subsequently halted the payment. Neither the school nor the recipient ever questioned my decision—they knew better.

The school administration that sat in on the grant reviews was a total embarrassment. On one such meeting with Z. Smith Reynolds, I was so taken aback from the behavior of the college, I wished my chair had been poised over a trap door.

After several years of working so hard and garnering awards, we were no longer the partner Z. Smith Reynolds sought. Instead of Race

GOING BACK HOME TO VISIT

Will Not Divide Us, race was clearly now a wall. We had proved the community and local government leaders right—all along they said we were a school that catered to white kids between the ages of 18-22, *racially sensitive only when convenient.* Our program folded.

Despite the professional disappointment, the personal rewards were immeasurable. My grade school daughter, Summer, had spent her after-school hours in my office, had been invited to perform Native American Dance at the Hmong New Year, passed out bike helmets to the Latino community children, and sat on the front row during one of author Maya Angelou's lectures.

During her dance at the Hmong New Year celebration held at the fairgrounds, her moccasins slipped on the slick canvas and she fell. The culturally unaware audience thought it was part of the act and roared with laughter. Instead of running off in tears to the side, she picked herself up, got back in rhythm and raised her eyes to the sky in gratitude when her performance was over.

During this same time there was another little girl in her class who had spent joyous months bullying Summer. I did the normal parenting chat. Ask to go to the end of the line so she can't poke you in the back or stomp on your shoes; let your teacher know. The situation did not improve so I decided to pop in for lunch one day just for observation or parental due diligence. I wanted to make sure I was getting the full story.

The bully, undeterred, was even brazen in her comments to me. A week later I dressed Summer in a brand-new gray knit A-line dress with a matching bow sewn to the bodice. That afternoon, I joined the other hundred parents in the carpool lane. As I approached Summer, she was holding the bow in her hand, which had been ripped off by her tormentor.

She opened the back door of my Lincoln and was almost instantaneously swallowed up by the huge back seat.

She snapped on her seat belt. "You know, momma," she said, "Lorne just won't let Martin Luther King's dream come true."

My daughter understood.

19
FINAL THOUGHTS

I'm not for one minute endorsing British colonialism, but starvation was nearly nonexistent during the breadbasket years of Rhodesia and the early days of Zimbabwe. Even during months of drought, there were subsidies delivered, even to the most remote schools.

I was there. I witnessed it. Fifty-pound bags of mealie meal and dried milk trucked to places that were hell on earth. Colonialism and missionaries brought education to Africa. Eighty percent of the people of my beloved country were literate. Rhodesia attained quality medical care for everyone and was light years ahead of most African nations.

What happened after President Robert Mugabe stepped into power in Rhodesia can be described as nothing less than catastrophic. An annihilation of thousands of people, the decimation of a once stable economy, food shortages for even the bare necessities, and destitution for those who survived.

It was gruesome. More than 30,000 people lost their lives. The late British Prime Minister Margaret Thatcher, Lord Soames and those who negotiated the peaceful transition of white to black power, destroyed a successful nation, reducing it to Third World status.

The Brits have a history of creating horrific holocausts outside of their imperial borders and then expecting their colonists to fall into line and participate when they experience an hour of need.

HOTDOGS FOR HYENAS

Lord Kitchener created his scorched earth policy in the second Boer War (1899-1902) in South Africa, where 28,000 Boers died in British concentration camps, 26,000 women and children (of whom more than 22,000 were under the age of 16), 1,700 men over the age of 16, and another 1,400 elderly persons perished. No one was ever held accountable and there were never any apologies.

Nearly 15 years later, Britain called on South Africans to serve during World War I. It could be surmised that South Africa had few reasons to join forces with Britain—many believed that a British defeat would bring about the end of British dominance in Africa.

But the bonds remained strong between the two countries. Amazingly, 136,000 South Africans fought for Britain in the Middle East and Western Front. Beloved General Jan Smuts and soldier-statesman Louis Botha conquered German-held Southwest Africa. This was considered to be one of the most successful campaigns of the Great War. Smuts was later put in charge of the conquest of German East Africa.

In the end, nearly a quarter of a million South Africans supported allied troops and 18,600 South Africans died in World War I. Right next door in Southern Rhodesia, soldiers paid their own way to England to join the British Army. Troopers were known for their excellent marksmanship on the Western Front.

Southern Rhodesia contributed more manpower to the British war effort than any other dominion or colony—more than Britain itself. White troops numbered 5,716, about 40% of the white men in the colony, with 1,720 of these serving as commissioned officers. The Rhodesia Native Regiment enlisted 2,507 black soldiers. Few in the West acknowledge or understand the people of Africa's participation and commitment to victory during the World Wars. Over 26,000 Southern Rhodesians of all races served in World War II.

Rhodesian-born Prime Minister Ian Smith, a decorated World War II pilot, survived a nighttime air crash, only to go right back into combat after his broken jaw and facial injuries healed. Yet when he called on Britain for understanding in 1965 as he stood

FINAL THOUGHTS

firm in declaring independence, Britain, instead of assisting, was the gunship against this tiny landlocked country. They were the muscle men behind the declaration of international sanctions, bringing the entire United Nations on board to bring down Rhodesia. The U.S. sided with Britain, yet at this exact period of time both Rhodesians and South Africans were serving in the Vietnam War.

The reason? Southern Africa could see how communism would spread and infect their successful and growing economies, devastating the infrastructure of the countries.

How insightful was that? Rhodesia, once a country with rich and successful mining operations, has now been gobbled up by the Chinese government. Zimbabwe's lithium deposits are second to none in Africa. Lithium, known as "white oil," is an essential component in the production of high-tech equipment and batteries for electric vehicles. With Zimbabwe's ability to meet 20% of the world's demand for lithium ore, China has invested heavily into this market—while the U.S. looks elsewhere.

Missionaries, Service and Opportunities

You can accurately conclude that I possess a jaundiced view of missions. My outlook is not skewed because of something I have read, a week at a missions retreat, or a church program honoring the "mission of the month" club.

In my sedate years, I have had the opportunity to participate in my church-sponsored mission trips. I encouraged my daughter to also participate in mission trips. But I guarantee you that on these trips, the others were oblivious to the intense pain I endured as a young woman at the hands of a corrupt mission organization.

In many walks of life, there are the competent and sincere contributors (the givers) and at the other end of the spectrum the selfish users (the takers). I believe that if Jesus walked among us today and was called to be a missionary, it is possible a church board or unqualified missions committee would be evaluating his resume and likely question his sincerity.

And I know that once on the field, Jesus's style of ministering to others might be decimated by others due to jealousy or their own ineptness. I'm certainly not comparing my family to Jesus, but there are those on the field who did not practice the Ten Commandments or follow Jesus's leadership from the Sermon on the Mount. I've witnessed missionaries that are neither heavenly bound nor earthly good.

We need to rethink how we serve people. For generations, missionaries have been commissioned to go to all corners of the earth. The Great Commission. It has all been singularly channeled in a conduit going in one direction regardless if it's medical, educational or evangelical.

In 1736, John Wesley arrived in Georgia to spread God's word to Native Americans. Wesley was typical in his mission approach to indigenous people. First there is a calling, then an assessment of skills, and finally a commitment to serve. Wesley wrote in his journal, "I went to America, to convert the Indians; but oh! who shall convert me?" Rarely do we ask, "What will the people teach *me*?"

The reports through newsletters and furloughs back to America typically share how many children have been educated, what the building projects and budgets look like, what diseases are being treated, what additional medical supplies, equipment, and staff are needed, how many have been baptized or led to Christ and how many churches have been established. In our arrogance we rarely share with colleagues or supporters how those we were sent to serve affected and influenced our lives.

Are we doing others a service when we haven't figured out how we will help others sustain what we've brought to them, when the role of the missionary, the Doctors Without Borders, or government programs are gone? How have we worked with existing traditional healers to see how we can blend local medicines with western medicines?

How can they understand one God when they may have several? Do we even know the names of their deities and their importance to their culture? Once again, we enter countries with our over-abundance

FINAL THOUGHTS

of book learning and tell another culture what they have to contribute is wiped clean because we know better. What's the message we are sending? Should we just be sending, or should we be sending and receiving? Why do we think we have the perfect message?

In the early years of living in the bush we observed babies brought to us for treatment (usually for diarrhea) had the fontanel slathered with cow dung and left to dry, leaving a hard crust. It looked like a bowl of eczema. This was appalling; why would they do this? Before treating the baby for whatever the ailment, we would scrub their heads clean. The next time they returned, there would be a fresh application of cow dung on the soft spot. After a few years, Dad said, "It's not really hurting anything, is it? If they say it's protecting the soft spot and bringing the skull together, then leave it alone."

We never did explore if there was anything medicinal in the cow crap. We never asked how long and where they began this practice. We also never knew if there were other indigenous medicines added to this mixture. We were accepting because we didn't want to fight, but we also weren't *curious*.

As the years went by and we introduced formal education, the now-educated parents would bring their children to us with cute bonnets and clean heads.

Why no cow dung? "It's not clean."

Where did they learn that? Did we deliver a message that had no value? Within one generation we had discouraged a practice without appropriate explanation or replacement.

According to Robert and Michele Root-Bernstein, "Any natural substance or folk therapy that has survived for centuries has a high probability of yielding an effective clinical treatment. Thus, the trial-and-error of folk medicine provides an important resource for modern research. Indeed, we can prime the pump of modern medical innovation by exploiting time-honored medical practices of the past." (Root-Bernstein, 1997)

Was the cow dung a part of medicine's evolutionary process? I have no idea. But like so many practices and approaches in missions, we scrub our patients and converts clean, imposing our righteous values on other cultures without asking why.

Before Zimbabwe's independence in 1980, life expectancy for the people was 64 years old. During the reign of President Mugabe, the life expectancy of its citizens plummeted to 39 years.

In the past 10+ years the incidence of cancers in Zimbabwe has skyrocketed. During the 2016 ASCO (American Society of Clinical Oncology) Annual Meeting, Oncologist Webster Kadzatsa, MD and Eric Chokunonga presented "The Status and Challenges of Cancer Care in Zimbabwe." (Kadzatsa, 2016)

Zimbabwe has one of the few functional national cancer registries in Africa, which was established in 1985. As Zimbabwe's screening, diagnostics, and therapeutic capabilities improve during the next few decades, the incidence rates of most cancers are expected to increase as life-expectancy is restored. As citizens age, the risk for the development of most cancers increases. With a population of nearly 15 million, 6,548 cancers were diagnosed in 2013, the most recent year for which statistics are available.

The study reports: "When a comparison is made between the statistics for black Zimbabweans and non-black Zimbabweans, our cancer registry data show that a higher proportion of non-black patients are diagnosed with colon cancer as compared to black patients. However, black Zimbabweans are diagnosed at a younger age than non-black Zimbabweans. It was also noted that black patients were more likely to be diagnosed with colon cancer when referred for a colonoscopy as compared to non-black patients. These differences can be attributed to the varying population age structures, access to health care services, and lifestyle and dietary patterns.

"The use of alternative medicine is high among patients with cancer worldwide. Herbal treatment and faith healing are common practices in Zimbabwe. The National Cancer Control Committee has made efforts to try and engage traditional healers, herbalists, and other complementary and alternative medicine practitioners in

FINAL THOUGHTS

order to reduce the late presentation of some patients with cancer to conventional medicine."

According to Kadzatsa and Chokunonga, "In September 2015 ASCO and the College of Health Sciences of the University of Zimbabwe conducted a 3-day Multidisciplinary Cancer Management Course focusing on breast, colon and head and neck cancers. After this meeting, the quality of our MDTB meetings has greatly improved."

Unfortunately, brain drain remains a huge problem in Zimbabwe and cancer treatment is a specialized field. Citizens trained in medical disciplines are in high demand across the world. High-income countries tend to benefit most from outer labor migration and Zimbabwe tends to lose its most experienced medical physicists, radiologists, and oncologists, resulting in the weakening of its systems that are still in developmental infancy.

So how can western practitioners and professionals assist Zimbabwe? Partnerships must be established. Diplomacy will go a long way. It's important to bring hope and relief to the overworked and understaffed medical specialists. Instead of plunging into costly cancer care as Zimbabweans are diagnosed with the preventable colon cancer, initiate programs such as screening colonoscopy. Sending teams of primary care physicians and techs to train primary care physicians in Zimbabwe to perform Tandem (team) Colonoscopy could ease the burden. Using mission schools and clinics for educating the community can be a rich resource for both the training and subsequent provisions of services. Other key bridges that would be invaluable would be to:

- Develop relationships with Ngangas' and traditional healers
- Create relationships with *kraal* heads (elders)
- Develop mentorship and education programs through the use of Zoom or other interactive applications
- Create community outreach educational programs such as the film nights we introduced years ago

I'm a solutionist. With the rapid progression and availability to communicate with one another nearly anywhere in the world, there are opportunities for virtual round tables and consults. Partnering with retired physicians, educators and business partners from America would be a godsend to Zimbabwe as they exchange their years of expertise and sage wisdom. During his 1992 visit to South Africa, President Bill Clinton, stated, "Not what we can do for Africa. What we can do *with* Africa."

I fully understand that America has been skeptical of investing on any level, (healthcare, tourism, education, and business) in Zimbabwe and rightfully so. But, in the 1960s, when the time was perfect, America turned its back. Zimbabwe slid down the crooked path of so many African countries: corruption, trillion-dollar bills, despots, and voter suppression.

This tiny landlocked country, home of the Great Zimbabwe Ruins and Victoria Falls, is ancient. It is not a country of genetic deficiencies, as my dad fiercely fought mission power brokers over. The schools we built are still operating as well as the clinic. These and other facilities throughout the country need our help.

As author Graham Hancock said, "We are a species with amnesia." But we don't have to acquiesce to amnesia. There are needs in this country and there are solutions that can be met to rebuild this once great nation…my Zimbabwe.

Our Zimbabwe
Henry Olonga

This land our land, is our Zimbabwe
A land of peace for you and me
Once born in pain and segregation
But now we live in harmony

Now flies the flag, our nation's glory
We live with pride inside our hearts
As we all stand to build our nation
This is our land, our Zimbabwe

Though I may go to distant borders
My heart will yearn for this my home
For time and space may separate us
And yet she holds my heart alone

Now flies the flag, my nation's glory
I'll live with pride inside my heart
I'll make a stand to build this nation
This is my land, my Zimbabwe

Now flies the flag our nation's glory
We'll live with pride inside our hearts
As we all stand to build our nation
This is our land, our Zimbabwe

YouTube: Our Zimbabwe Henry Olonga

EPILOGUE

In 2016, one of the last Central Africa Mission missionaries still living contacted me asking me to intercede on his behalf to arrange a meeting with my parents. My parents were gracious but said that a meeting was not necessary. They wanted to be left alone and leave the past where it was. This elder missionary contacted me again in 2017 with the same results.

After several months, he reached out again. Finally, my parents responded. They would welcome this also-aging missionary into their home. He proposed that he and his wife would drive the 15 hours to my parents' home in Florida.

Upon their arrival, Dad told them, "Today there will be no malice; there will be no harsh words. There is no place for this in our home. This will be a spirit-filled visit full of love." Mum, ever gracious, already had the table laden with a three-course meal for all of them.

This Godly missionary shed tears during the meeting. He acknowledged that missionaries Pemberton and Pruett, the power-brokers of Central Africa Mission, had been behind the ousting of my dad from his mission and the country he loved. He explained how the organization had set up Dad's arrest at the airport; how they'd manipulated and made promises to other missionaries in order to have control of the beautiful mission schools and clinic my family had built; how they'd tried to force the missionaries to sign a document falsely stating that Dad had taken money from them (a document the visiting missionary had refused to sign); and how the personal attack on Mum had been accomplished. This final admission we had always suspected, but there had never been enough proof.

The end result was that the two individuals were absolutely determined to be as destructive as possible, regardless of the cost or the ripple effect it had on all of us. My sense of place was destroyed by them. But even more devastating, my mum nearly lost her life.

After the meeting, the elder missionary wrote to me saying it was difficult to know if any "healing took place" that day. He went on to say that because he was a member of Central Africa Mission, his association was "suspected" to have contributed to the anguish my family lived through.

My parents' reaction was quite different. "Today, we finally had confirmation of what happened," Dad said. "You could say that it was forty years too late, but it wasn't. We all experienced healing and sweet, sweet fellowship."

Several weeks after the meeting, Mum called me to say she had received a thank-you note from the missionaries. She said, "I have decided I am going to write a letter back, because I really want to stay in contact with them."

What an example of forgiveness Mum exuded at ninety-four years of age. My parents both give God the glory that Dad has learned to loosen and throw away the nails others intentionally drove into him. He has forgiven. He is forgiven. There is no negotiation with God. The ground at the foot of the cross is level.

Recently, I was asked to play at a funeral for a dear friend. The family had selected "When Peace Like a River." After I felt I had mastered it on my fiddle, I called my parents and played it for them.

Dad began to sing along, but halfway through his voice choked with tears, overrunning his beautiful tenor voice. With great difficulty I played to the end and put the phone back up to my ear.

We cried together as we revisited the deep connection this song has for us and how it is still being used to bring peace to others, including our family. Despite all, it is still true.

It is well. It is well with my soul…

Three generations of hands—Mum's, Dad's, my daughter's and mine—on a tablecloth Mum made in the bush and brought back to America.

ACKNOWLEDGMENTS

Graham David "Bob" and Denise Gawler

Bob and Denise were our closest neighbors in the Lowveld of the Rhodesian bush. Bob ranched Section 8 (233,000 acres) of Liebigs Ranch, massive cattle holding totaling a million and a quarter acres. Bob and Denise were my alternate set of parents, they were my aunt and uncle, they were my mentors, and more than anything, they were my best friends. Often, we would spend the night in their guest room sleeping on freshly ironed sheets.

Before we built our first water reservoir for drinking and swimming, they made sure that I was at their place often. They lived on top of a *kopje* (granite outcropping) with a spectacular panoramic view of their ranch. They had terraced gardens that tumbled fragrances of bougainvillea, flamboyant trees and bananas. Behind their house Bob built a circular concrete water tank, 20 feet in diameter, that also served as a swimming pool. As youngsters at 10 and 12 years old, my brother and I would ride the 25 miles on our motorcycle to cool off from the intense Lowveld heat. There is nothing like swimming at night under the stars of Africa. The water in the concrete tank was warm and soothing. As we floated on our backs, the stars felt like they were within our arm's reach.

I learned to inoculate 1,000 head of cattle for black leg under Bob's tutelage. After a hearty breakfast of eggs, *boerewors* and fried toast cooked over the open fire, we would move to the wire shoots reaching in with a syringe to work as quickly as we could. Some calves would be in such a rush they would climb up on top of one another causing a bovine log jam. "Careful," Bob would say. "Make sure you inoculate correctly near the neck. Don't want an abscess to develop at the needle site." The Argentinian owned Liebigs imported semen from Texas, shipped to Rhodesia for their white Brahmans. I quickly learned about artificial insemination, which was an advantage in my adult years in the horse industry using AI on my mares.

Bob taught me where deadly venomous *boom slangs* (Afrikaans for tree snake) would be hanging, how to shoot a leopard in a trap (one that had been killing local cattle) and how to dance the waltz at my first big Old Year's Night party. Bob's colorful background extended from car racing at the adrenaline end of the spectrum to supervising in the copper mines in Northern Rhodesia (Zambia). He always had a fascinating yarn to spin. He knew Africa, He *was* Africa.

South African by birth, he was especially at home in the bush. His everyday dress was tan khaki shorts and shirt with brown mining boots—boots that had two buckles at the side mid-calf and bright emerald green thick soles with treads. My brother loved them so much that Bob bought him a pair. As a marksman, few were Bob's match.

The attribute that endeared him to others was his fairness. His kindness and generosity were legend. He was the consummate gentleman rising to his feet any time a woman entered the room. He was a friend to everyone who had the pleasure of his company. He was educated in boarding schools and spoke eloquently, but there was a devilish streak to him. Born Graham David Gawler, he earned the nickname Bob due to boundless energy, jumping up and down like a sewing machine bobbin from the time he could walk.

Denise was the ultimate hostess. She had a *Mazoe* orange drink or a lime and water in my hands before I even got through the door. She was an excellent seamstress; I could sketch a frock freehand, and Denise would have it made by nightfall.

We spent many holidays together. I had my first exposure to alcohol under their watchful eye during my later teens. During a party that was attended by a little too "polished" Portuguese gentleman several years older than me, Bob kept a watchful eye across the room, ready to castrate the bloke if a line appeared to be crossed. He never told my parents.

Bob also smoothed the feathers of my brother when we were on holiday in the KwaZulu Natal. We were staying at cottages near the beach. Our waiter, who was of Indian descent, wanted my address so he could write to me. I told him I would leave my address under my napkin. My brother was alarmed and told me how much trouble I would be in because of apartheid and he was going to tell my parents. Bob swooped in and assured everyone that no harm was done.

Bob and Denise were the last friends I said goodbye to whenever I left for trips to America and the first I rushed through the bush to see on my return. We always embraced with genuine kisses, both hello and goodbye. They produced four of the finest daughters any parent could dream of. Bob built them a "Wendy House" (playhouse/schoolhouse) behind the main house, where Denise schooled them for a couple years before it was time to send them off to boarding school.

Bob and Denise stayed in Rhodesia until it was no longer safe at their isolated homestead on the *kopje*. They, like my parents, moved to what they considered safer countries—my parents to an area where the borders of Zimbabwe, South Africa and Botswana on the Limpopo River joined. Bob and Denise moved to the Natal (KwaZulu) in South Africa.

We were all in a state of shock when my mother was attacked by terrorists and left for dead on their farm. My parents hadn't moved far enough away to escape the rampant violence. Bob and Denise lived in the calm of St. Martin's Sugar Estates in the KwaZulu (Natal) for years.

Their three oldest daughters came to stay with me when I lived in Washington, D.C. Before the era of social media, our correspondence consisted of thin blue aerogram letters and annual Christmas cards. In the summer of 2017, I received a call that there had been an attack on the kindest man I'd ever known. The locks of Bob and Denise's front gate had been broken. Denise, who was recuperating from knee surgery and had limited mobility, was tied up in her bed. She was helpless as Bob was brutally murdered. He was 82.

They had lived 30 years beyond what was the worst of the violent bush wars in Rhodesia only to become a statistic in the planned farm attacks systematically annihilating white farmers in South Africa. We were all stunned and sickened by this and will forever miss him.

Bob's favorite words to me were, "That's champion!" Bob and Denise, you are forever champions in my heart.

Graham David "Bob" Gawler

Jimius Ndlovu

Jimius was everything to my family. I don't remember when he was hired by my parents, but it seemed like he had always been with us. He worked for my mother in the house, he was a translator at the clinic, and, on Sunday, he was a preacher at one of the sites on Maranda Tribal Trust.

Jimius taught me the Ndebele language—his first language (Sendebele as we said in the bush). I was bored with Shona, but Ndebele was exciting—remarkable for the distinctive clicks in the language. Depending on where you clicked, from the roof of your mouth, or in the front behind your top teeth, or the inside of your cheek, it all means something unique and is spelled differently. For instance, in the "nc" in *ncube* (zebra), the lips are brought together, and the tongue clicks the roof of the mouth just behind the front teeth.

Ambitiously, every day we spoke to each other in different languages. We had a notebook with the days of the week. Every day a new word in that day's language was written in the notebook and we would challenge each other. Monday was Afrikaans (I lived in what was called an Afrikaans-speaking district); Tuesday, Shona; Wednesday, Ndebele; Thursday a combo of Fanagalo and Shangaan; and Friday, English.

HOTDOGS for HYENAS

My mother had a rule that breakfast had to be finished by 7:30 so the floors could be polished. Our floors were typical concrete with a top smooth skim coat of color added. Most floors in Southern African homes had dark green or red skim coats, but my parents decided to be more dramatic. We used a black powder to color the concrete.

Floors were given a fresh coat of Cobra wax every Monday morning. The smell of the fresh wax wafting through the house was indicative of what day of the week it was: Monday, laundry, floors, and curry and rice for lunch. Yes, the floors were stunning, but the black wax dyed the bottoms of our feet and for kids who never wore shoes, our feet generally looked dirty. I would come running through the lounge door, past the corner fireplace with the extended seating area, heading towards the dining room. Many times, the floor cleaning was already in progress.

We never missed a beat. Jimius and I began the language of the day immediately. He was 5'11" — tall, strong, with an infectious grin. His most prized possession was the watch my mother bought him. He made sure it was visible in every photo taken of him.

With a Standard Six (eighth-grade) education, Jimius was well schooled for that time. He could have taught primary school if he had had the opportunity to attend the teachers college in Bulawayo. My parents offered to send him, but he refused, saying he would rather work for the mission.

Following the birth of his first child, he asked me to name her. I did: Stella. It was an incredible honor to be asked to name a child, particularly at my age. I spent so much time under the African night sky this was a natural choice of name for his newborn daughter.

When the first man walked on the moon in 1969, I said, "Jimius there are men walking on the moon."

Jimius said, "Right now?" It was daylight, but we could still see the faint outline of the moon. We both peered at the moon as if we would be able to see them.

"Yes!" I said.

JIMIUS NDLOVU

Jimius had picked up a few of my expressions and responded, "Pretty cool," but immediately continued. "Explain how they do not fall off?"

Later in the day, he came to me with a brilliant idea.

"Can we meet them?"

"Meet who?" I asked.

"Let's get in the airplane (our single-engine Cessna 206) and go up there to the moon and meet them."

When Jimius saw a photo of me after being in university for one year, he announced to my mother that I must come home *now now* for I "looked *too too* white." And when I did come back the next year, he was waiting for me.

I will always have a special place in my heart for Jimius Ndlovu. He tattled on me a time or two. One time, I had designed a sun dress and made my own pattern. I thought the orange and white knit number was pretty edgy with a V-neck, V-back and matching Vs under the arms. The shoulder straps were attached with little silver buttons. I learned to sew on a treadle sewing machine and in no time my creation was complete. I tried it on. Perfect.

Jimius went to my mother and said, "I think Missy Pamela's dress has too many points," referring to the Vs. Mum looked at the V-neckline and agreed it was more plunging than it should be. I had to stich the seam a little higher.

Jimius was non-political, but he had one mark against him. He was Ndebele. He was therefore targeted by the ZANU PF party (the party of dictator Robert Mugabe). They intentionally set out to annihilate the Ndebele. The worst blood bath in Zimbabwe's history wasn't during the 15-year war of liberation—it came later as Mugabe consolidated power in Zimbabwe and established his *Gukurahundi* (Shona phrase that means "the wind that wipes away trash").

This facet of the Mugabe government from 1983 to 1987 not only led to the deaths of thousands of Ndebele citizens, but also entrenched the rift of tribalism with the country pitting the Mashona against the Ndebele. The massacres have been blamed squarely on the

Jimius Ndlovu with his wife and daughter Stella.
His watch over Stella is ever present in photos.

shoulder of then-President Robert Mugabe who is believed to have ordered the genocide to eliminate his opposition, Joshua Nkomo.

Tens of thousands of Ndebeles were killed during the *Gukurahundi*, waged by the Zimbabwe Defense Force's North Korean-trained Fifth Brigade. The Fifth Brigade would march into Ndebele villages, round up anyone suspected or accused of being anti-ZANU, and force them to dig their own graves before executing them. Conservative estimates put the number of civilian deaths around 8,000, but Ndebele sources insist it was closer to 30,000.

My beloved friend Jimius was among them. When I was told that he had been slaughtered in the most unthinkable way by Mugabe's thugs, I wept.

And the daughter I named? I heard she might be at several locations but, so far, I have been unsuccessful in finding her.

Jimius, you did not tell me *Chisarai* – "I am leaving, but you are staying here." I would have given anything to see your hair turn grey and listen to your wisdom.

Bibliography

Hemingway, Ernest. 1935. *Green Hlls of Africa*. New York: Charles Scribner.

Kadzatsa, Webster. 2016. *The Status and Challenges of Cancer Care in Zimbabwe*. San Francisco: ASCO.

Lindsay, Vachel. 1914. *The Congo*. New York.

Pollock, D.C., Ruth E. Van Reken, and Michael V. Pollock. 2009. *Third Culture Kids: Growing Up Among Worlds*. New York: Nicholas Brealey.

The Rhodesian Herald. 1965-79. Salisbury, Rhodesia. Argus Print and Publishing.

Root-Bernstein, Robert and Michele. 1997. *Honey, Mud, Maggots, and Other Medical Marvels: The Science Behind Folk Remedies and Old Wives' Tales*. Boston: Houghton Mifflin.

Schweitzer, Albert. 1933. *Out of My Life and Thought*. New York: Holt.

Smith, Ian Douglas. 1997. *The Great Betrayal*. London: Blake.

Useem, John and Ruth Hill. 1996. "Adult Third Culture Kids." *Strangers at Home*. Aletheia Publcation.

Interviews

Courtney, Frances V. Interview 2020.

Courtney, Thomas N. Interviews 2015-2018.

Courtney, Michael T. Interviews 2015-2017.

Morley, Linda. Interviews 2015-2018.

ABOUT THE AUTHOR

PAMELA COURTNEY'S most formative years were spent growing up in the bush of Africa. Inter-cultural and multi-lingual, Pamela is truly a Third-Culture Kid/Adult. Having lived or traveled in 52 countries, Pamela has always stood on the principle that it's important to travel before your medication gets heavier than your luggage. In 2016, she traveled to the UK and hiked Hadrian's Wall by herself. This coast-to-coast 85-mile trek took her five days.

Pamela received a BS in Recording Industry Management (business side) from Middle Tennessee State University and a MA from East Tennessee State University. The Archives of Appalachia houses 1,400 pages and recordings of Pamela's research on Appalachia (the Pamela Courtney Collection) while at ETSU. She completed her graduate work while restoring an 1825 log house, being a golf/soccer mom, running a small farm raising Texas Longhorns and Tennessee Walking Mules and creating an archaeological dig site for local students.

Pamela is passionate about bringing an end to health disparities in colon cancer testing for African Americans. She recently wrote an article for publication through the Society of Gastroenterology Nurses and Associates (SGNA) reinforcing the urgency for change.

Pamela co-authored three books before completing *Hot Dogs for Hyenas*. She resides in Columbia, South Carolina.

You can visit her at

pamelacourtney.com

www.ingramcontent.com/pod-product-compliance
Lightning Source LLC
Chambersburg PA
CBHW050314120526
44592CB00014B/1904